When Mothers
Go to Jail

When Mothers Go to Jail

Ann M. Stanton
Arizona State University
School of Law

LexingtonBooks
D.C. Heath and Company
Lexington, Massachusetts
Toronto

Library of Congress Cataloging in Publication Data

Stanton, Ann M
    When mothers go to jail.

    Bibliography: p.
    Includes index.
    1. Children of women prisoners—United States. 2. Maternal deprivation.
3. Women prisoners—Legal status, laws, etc.—United States. 4. Children—
Legal status, laws, etc.—United States. I. Title.
HV8886.U5S7   362.8'2   79-3522
ISBN 0-669-03461-4

Copyright © 1980 by D.C. Heath and Company

Published simultaneously in Canada

Printed in the United States of America

International Standard Book Number: 0-669-03461-4

Library of Congress Catalog Card Number: 79-3522

Contents

List of Figures
and Tables

Preface

During my second year of law school, I had the chance to accompany an attorney to a local county jail, where he was to interview a client brought in the night before on narcotics charges. This was my first exposure to the inner workings of the penal system, that is, an attorney-client session inside a jail.

The client was a 28-year-old woman without a prior arrest record. The interview was conducted in a small, makeshift office off the booking area, where it was difficult to ignore the continuous noise coming from activities outside. The woman was anxiously awaiting a visit from her mother, whom she had called as soon as she had been arrested. When the discussion turned to potential plea-bargain options, I excused myself, offering to check with the deputy on duty about visiting procedures.

I found the mother and her grandson standing in the poorly lit waiting area. The woman was obviously unsettled and kept repeating how upsetting this experience must be for the boy. She said this over and over again, but I noticed throughout our conversation that the child remained impassive, something of an enigma.

When the official visiting time came, I walked with them and other visitors to the designated section, a room divided by a wall of bulletproof glass. The visitors settled into assorted folding chairs beside separate telephone sets along the counter for talking to the prisoners on the other side of the glass partition.

Discussing this case later with the attorney, I learned the woman had pled guilty to reduced charges and had received a six-month sentence. When I inquired what consideration the court had given to the child's welfare, he said the subject had not arisen during the hearing.

This experience aroused my curiosity and concern about what happens to children when their mothers are sent to jail. Studies on maternal deprivation have typically dealt with children in orphanages, with children experiencing wartime separations, and more recently with those hospitalized for long periods. Very little has been written on separation due to the incarceration of a parent. My experience persuaded me that children separated from incarcerated parents would be an interesting area of research, which might contribute some insights to separation experiences and useful information to an ignored area of our penal system.

Acknowledgments

Special thanks are due to Eleanor E. Maccoby, who provided much guidance and good counsel throughout the course of this study, and to Robert R. Sears for his initial support in this research project. I am grateful to Albert H. Hastorf, Jr., director of the Boys Town Center, for his financial aid and to Michael S. Wald for his practical advice and assistance.

The project could not have been accomplished without the cooperative efforts of many individuals. I appreciate those efforts from the sheriffs, jail staffs, probation departments' personnel, school officials, and especially the mothers and children who participated in this study. I am also indebted to the interviewers: Peter Tovar, Barbara Miller, and especially Katherine Bistrup. Others who provided enthusiastic help with the project include Kristin Dean, Paul Matthews, and Susan Seidman. I had the skilled assistance of Joyce Sanders, Constance McKee, and Claudette Peterson, who transcribed many hours of taped interviews, and Mary Lou Brooks, Kay Ruhland and Alice Kleeman, who prepared the final manuscript. Finally, Robert Haddock and my brother, Michael Stanton, deserve special thanks for their advice and encouragement.

This research project was made possible by a grant from the Boys Town Center for the Study of Youth Development, an interdisciplinary research institute at Stanford University, and by a financial award from the Soroptimist Federation of the Americas. I am also grateful to the National Science Foundation for its early support of my graduate studies in psychology.

When Mothers
Go to Jail

1 Introduction

Children begin by loving their parents; as they grow older they judge them; sometimes they forgive them.   —Oscar Wilde

Children of imprisoned offenders are the hidden victims of a criminal lifestyle. Yet there is little reliable literature that describes the consequences for a child whose parent is incarcerated or considers the effects this experience has on the child.

An estimated 15,000 women are incarcerated in the United States on any one day (Koontz, 1971; Glick & Neto, 1977). Approximately 56 percent of these women are mothers who had dependent children living with them immediately prior to incarceration (Glick & Neto, 1977). These children are almost always separated from their mothers, and the community accepts such separation as an inevitable consequence of imprisonment. But mother-child separation upon incarceration has not always been common practice.

In the 1700s the prisons of England permitted mothers to keep their children with them (Smith, 1962). Female criminals who were transported from Britain to Australia in the early 1800s were accompanied by their children under the age of 7. By 1850, English prisons no longer permitted children to stay with their mothers, but infants born in prison were allowed to remain until they were 6 years old (Smith, 1962).

In more recent times certain foreign countries have provided special arrangements for children of incarcerated mothers. Mexican children sometimes live with their mothers in prison (Teeters, 1944) or in penal colonies where autonomous villages are established for entire families (DeFord, 1962). In Colombia, inmates' children on occasion have been cared for in special facilities, and in Ecuador younger children sometimes remain with their mothers (Teeters, 1946). West Germany's largest women's penitentiary permits children up to 3 years old to stay with their mothers; day care is provided while the mothers work. In Denmark, pregnant inmates keep their children in a prison nursery for up to two years (McWhinnie, 1961). In Yugoslavia, some inmates and their infants stay in a special home until the children are a year old. The children are then placed with relatives or in an institution, while the mother serves the remainder of her sentence (DeFord, 1962). While these arrangements may be neither characteristic of these countries in general nor necessarily desirable, they illustrate alternatives to complete separation.

1

Early in this century a few American institutions permitted infants to remain with their mothers. In the 1920s, for example, several training facilities for delinquent girls had infants on the premises (Reeves, 1929). But the predominant American practice has been to exclude children as quickly as possible. At some institutions pregnant inmates are transferred to hospitals in the local communities so that children are not stigmatized by being born in prison (Monahan, 1941; Zemans & Cole, 1948; Johnson, 1969). Some state institutions have nurseries to temporarily care for babies born during a woman's incarceration until an outside placement can be arranged. These transient accommodations range in duration from a few days to as long as three months.

Some American facilities have not allowed children under 16 or 18 years old to visit their incarcerated mothers because it is believed to be too traumatic for the children. Even mothers who have not been convicted, and are merely awaiting trial, are sometimes denied visitation (Burkhart, 1973). At other institutions such as the Nebraska Women's Reformatory and Minnesota Correctional Institution for Women, children are encouraged to visit and are allowed to spend an occasional weekend with their mothers (Bonfanti et al., 1974).

Concern for the maternal role of inmates seems to be growing in the United States. Several recommendations have been made to allow inmate mothers to keep their young children with them (Eyman, 1971; Palmer, 1972; National Institute of Law Enforcement and Criminal Justice, 1979). A number of residential facilities for mothers and children have recently been established (Glick & Neto, 1977) and others are under consideration. There is reason to believe that this developing interest in the relationship between the incarcerated mother and her children springs more from a concern for the mother's reform than for the children.

Advocates of penal reform, and particularly women's organizations, have focused on the plight of the incarcerated mother. Inmates and observers of jail life have noted that a forced separation from one's children constitutes serving truly "hard time" (Burkhart, 1973). Separation from family is frequently mentioned by inmate mothers as one of the most difficult aspects of incarceration (Ward & Kassebaum, 1965). Perhaps the harshest aspect of imprisonment for women is not the loss of liberty, but the separation from family and loss of the maternal role (Sykes, 1958; Giallombardo, 1966). Some commentators conclude that this separation generally constitutes more severe punishment for mothers than for fathers (Bonfanti et al., 1974; Ward & Kassebaum, 1965). Incarcerated fathers usually have wives who will care for their children, thus alleviating concern for the welfare of the children. Incarcerated mothers, by contrast, are often unmarried (Velimesis, 1969; Zalba, 1964) and consequently act alone in their responsibility to provide for their children.

Sometimes a mother's incarceration even raises questions about her future parental rights. A few legislatures (Florida, Illinois, Montana, New York, and Wyoming) provide that a parent's incarceration is sufficient, in and of itself, to permit termination of parental rights.[1] For example, *In the Matter of Anonymous* 79 Misc.2d 280, 359 N.Y.S.2d 738 (1974) a New York court found incarcerated parents suffer a loss of civil rights and are subject to statutory disabilities that qualify or eliminate the requirement of their consent to the adoption of their children.

The precise incidence of termination of parental rights due to incarceration is not known, but a study in Oregon (Lundberg et al., 1975) noted that prior imprisonment was the main reason for a mother's not living with her child at the time of arrest. The National Study of Women's Correctional Programs (Glick & Neto, 1977) found that prior incarceration of the mother doubled the incidence of children not living at home, from 16 percent for women who had never been in jail or prison before to 33 percent for those who had previously served time. It was not determined whether this difference resulted from court action or voluntary relinquishment.

Courts in a number of states have equated the imprisonment of a parent with an abandonment of parental responsibilities and implied the power to terminate parental rights upon incarceration [*Logan* v. *Coup.* 238 Md. 253, 208 A.2d 694 (1965); *In re Jaques*, 48 N.J. Super. 523, 138 A.2d 581 (1958)]. In contrast, several courts have stated or implied that abandonment is not established by incarceration alone.[2] Although incarceration per se is not always deemed sufficient to constitute abandonment, the fact of imprisonment may combine with other factors such as parental neglect and withholding of parental affection to lend support to a finding of abandonment [*In re Staat*, 287 Minn. 501, 178 N.W.2d 709 (1970)]. A Washington court considered the nature of the crime committed, the victim, the parent's inability to perform parental obligations because of imprisonment, and the parent's conduct prior to and during the sentence as relevant to finding parental unfitness [*In re Sego*, 82 Wash. 2d 736, 513 P.2d 831 (1973)]. In Oregon in *In re R* 543 P.2d 1096 (1975) the court held that a mother's continuing criminal conduct which often resulted in her being incarcerated established her unfitness and justified terminating her parental rights.

The recent interest in the problem of separation during incarceration has been encouraged by the increased emphasis modern corrections has placed on the utility of fostering inmate-family relationships for purposes of rehabilitation. Parole success (completion of parole without rearrest) is the common measure of rehabilitation; studies have repeatedly demonstrated a correlation between parole success and the existence of family ties for male offenders (Glaser, 1964; Holt & Miller, 1972; Morris, 1965; Zemans & Cavan, 1958). Supportive family relationships as shown by family visits and residence with the wife after release are related to lower recidivist rates. No parallel study has been reported associating familial factors with parole success for female offenders. Investigators have looked at incarcerated women's perceptions of the maternal role, and they recommend that recognition and enhancement of the maternal role in correction policies would "probably tend to promote rehabilitation as well as contribute to family solidarity" (Bonfanti et al., 1974).

The suggestion that intergenerational cycles of criminality exist has also contributed to the interest in the relationship of the incarcerated parent and child. It has even been suggested that delinquent women present a greater threat to society than many violent and dangerous men because of their potential to influence their children and possibly encourage them in criminal conduct (Gibbs, 1971). While there are no data indicating what percentage of offenders have children who also become offenders, studies have shown that many criminal offenders had parents who were convicted of crimes. Cloninger and Guze (1970) report that of 66 convicted female felons, 20 percent had had a father in jail or prison and an additional 9 percent had a mother who had been in jail or prison. In the present study 44 percent of the jailed mothers had parents and siblings who had been incarcerated; another 9 percent had only a parent incarcerated. In *Unraveling Juvenile Delinquency* (1950), the Gluecks report a very high correlation between male juvenile delinquency and parental criminality. McCord et al. (1959) report that children of criminal fathers tend to criminality, especially when other factors, such as instability of the mother, are present. In their study, 60 percent of the boys who had criminal mothers were delinquent themselves, and 67 percent of another group of thirty boys who had deviant mothers, defined as alcoholic or promiscuous, were also delinquent. These were significantly higher incidences of delinquency than for boys whose mothers were not criminal, alcoholic, or promiscuous. In a small fifteen-year follow-up study of children of male convicts in Oakland, California (Miller et al., 1972), children of convicts had more than four times as many records of deviance as did children in the normal control group. One-half of the children of convicts had a criminal arrest record. In addition, 26 percent of the mothers of these children also had criminal histories.

Interest in the separation of mother and child during incarceration is also generated by a humane concern for the children. But the general belief that children are adversely affected by such a separation is largely intuitive since the children have been virtually ignored by social scientists. In an attempt to understand the consequences of a parent's incarceration for children, this study describes the circumstances of incarcerated mothers and their children and explores the problems they encounter. Variables suggested in the psychological literature that could modify the effects of such incarceration on the families are examined. Two considerations in the study design were the effects of the separation on the mother-child relationship, and the child's legal socialization.

Since residential facilities for mothers and children are such a new and relatively rare phenomenon in the United States, it was not possible to collect data about the impact of such programs on children. This study was undertaken with no preconception about the relative merits of keeping the mother and child together versus separating them while the mother serves her sentence. However, information from this study provides comparisons between school-age children who are separated from their incarcerated mothers and children whose convicted mothers remain at home while on probation.

Notes

1. Fla. Stat. Ann. § 39.01 (Supp. 1971); Ill. Ann. Stat. Ch. 4 §§ 9.1-1, 9.1-8 (Smith-Hurd Supp. 1971); Mont. Rev. Codes Ann. § 61-205 (1947); N.Y. Dom Rel. Laws art. 7 § 111 (McKinney Supp. 1971); Wyo. Stat. Ann. § 1-710.2 (Supp. 1971).

2. Colorado: Diernfeld v. People 137 Colo. 238, 323 P.2d 628 (1958); Michigan: In re Kidder, 61 Mich. App. 451, 233 N.W.2d 495 (1975); Oregon: State v. Grady, 231 Or. 65, 371 P.2d 68 (1962); Pennsylvania: Adoption of Hall, 12 Mercer Co. L.J. 116 (1973); Farkas Adoption 62 Pa. D. & C.2d 488 (1973); Utah: In re State in interest of Valdez, 29 Utah 2d 63, 504 P.2d 1372 (1973).

2 Mother-Child Separation

Incarceration disrupts the parent-child relationship but very little is known about the effects of this separation upon the family unit or the mother-child relationship. However, studies of maternal and filial deprivation investigated the effects of separation under a variety of circumstances other than incarceration. Most research on attachment and separation has dealt primarily with infants and young children. This focus on young children is due in part to the finding that attachments usually develop within the first year of life and in part to a belief in the special significance of early life experiences on later development. Several theoretical orientations and methodological approaches have been used in studying maternal deprivation and have contributed to increasing knowledge about attachment and the effects of separation.

Bowlby's emphasis on the importance of attachment behavior and the need for a young child to form bonds with other people has been most influential in this area (1951, 1973). His writings reflect a psychoanalytic background and make extensive use of research in animal ethology. He asserts that to ensure mental health, an infant or young child requires an intimate and continuous attachment relationship. Bowlby also argues that there is a bias for a child to attach himself to one figure and this primary attachment or bond differs in kind from attachments to other people. Although this claim of a unique bond has been questioned, it remains an influential theory in the attachment literature (Rutter, 1972).

Also from a psychoanalytic tradition, Goldstein et al. (1973, 1979) advocate continuity as a primary guideline for decisions about child placement. They claim children of all ages need stability in their relationships, surroundings, and environmental influences for normal development.

When stressing the importance of continuity in the parent-child relationship, researchers generally point to three kinds of supporting evidence. First, young children experience stress and behavior disturbances immediately following separation from mothers as shown by experimental studies (Ainsworth & Bell, 1970; Maccoby & Feldman, 1972) and naturalistic observations (Yarrow, 1964). Second, clinical studies indicate the development of psychological disturbances after lengthy separation, and retrospective studies of people with personality disorders show a high percentage who had disturbances in their early family life, including a high incidence of separation (Bowlby, 1946, 1973). Third, a strong association

7

between "broken homes" and delinquency has been reported numerous times (Bowlby, 1946; Glueck & Glueck, 1950).

Although the association between delinquency and broken homes is frequently cited to demonstrate the negative long-term effects of separation, it is an oversimplification to attribute a high rate of delinquency to separation. Comparisons were made between three groups of boys: those with a deceased parent, those with divorced or separated parents, and those in intact families (Gibson, 1969; Glueck & Glueck, 1950). The incidence of delinquency was highest for boys whose parents were divorced or separated and only slightly increased for boys who had a decreased parent over the rate for boys from intact families. It is the absence of a stable home environment rather than the absence of a parent which is related to childhood delinquency (McCord et al., 1959). Research by the McCords shows significantly less juvenile delinquency from broken homes than from intact but quarrelsome and neglecting homes. Such findings bring the common assumption into question. It can be concluded that it is more likely family discord and the distortion of relationships with parents than the separation that predisposes problems in children's behavior. However, in spite of such findings, the association between broken homes or separation from a parent and delinquency is often cited to support the contention that a child requires a continuous relationship with adults and to argue that a child should not be separated from his parents, particularly his mother. Also commonly believed, but not adequately documented, is the idea that separation is more damaging to young children than to older children. It has been suggested that the younger a child is, the shorter the duration of separation he can endure without detrimental consequences (Bowlby, 1951; Goldstein et al., 1973).

Short separations of children from parents are not unusual or necessarily harmful. According to an English national sample, by the age of 5, a third of the children had been separated from their mothers for at least a week (Douglas et al., 1968). Short separations in early childhood are not usually associated with cognitive, emotional, or behavioral ill effects (Rutter, 1972). However, early childhood separations of over a month's duration and separations occurring in conjunction with family stress or discord have been associated with antisocial disorders and later deviant behavior (Ainsworth, 1962). It is difficult to draw meaningful conclusions from most of these studies because the causes of separation are undifferentiated, the child's age at the time of separation and the duration of the separation are not controlled, and the child's subsequent experiences are not taken into account.

Although there is variety in the theoretical orientations and research approaches, there is consensus that continuity in parent-child relationships is desirable. While some would not endorse the notion that the law's primary concern in child-custody decisions should be to protect the child's need for continuity, no one suggests that prolonged separation experiences are beneficial for young children. Indeed, the enforced separation of mothers or mother surrogates and children for lengthy periods is rarely approved in this society except under extraordinary circumstances. This discussion does not deal with the brief separations involved in daily substitute care.

One of the numerous difficulties confronting the researcher who wishes to study the naturally occurring separation of parents and children is the irregularity and infrequency of such occurrences in the normal course of childhood. Nor is it feasible to organize experimental studies in which children would be separated from their mothers at specific ages for varying periods of time under controlled conditions. Although there are ethical restraints to designing separation experiments with humans, extensive research with subhuman primates and other animals has investigated the long-lasting effects of early life separation experiences (Hinde & Spencer-Booth, 1971). A few studies were done with children involuntarily separated from their parents due to naturally arising causes, usually in emergency or crisis situations. Researchers looked at the effects of wartime separations on young children (Burlingham & Freud, 1942, 1944; Maas, 1963) and on family adjustment (Hill, 1949). Other research dealt with families in which a family member is committed to a mental institution or hospitalized (Groves, 1952; Schiff, 1965). Studies were also done in cases of separation and divorce (Despert, 1953; McDermott, 1970), and death of a parent (Cain & Fast, 1966). Investigations of these events are valuable sources of information about how children adjust to separation from parents.

Research on the children of offenders has been extremely limited and generally has considered male inmates and their families. British studies looked at families of imprisoned men (Morris, 1965) and women (Gibbs, 1971). An American study of family and marital adjustment of men committed to prison was done in Spokane County, Washington (Blackwell, 1959). The most extensive American study concerned with female prisoners and their children was done in California by Zalba (1964). This research concentrated on the relationships of the correctional institution and social agencies working with incarcerated women and their children. In addition to its value as a report on the shortcomings of community services, the study also revealed some of the problems that arise for children when a mother is imprisoned. None of these studies involving parental incarceration dealt directly with the children and their adjustment.

A few studies looked at the children themselves or at some performance measure of the children. Friedman and Esselstyn (1965) examined school performance and found that teachers rated children of imprisoned fathers as below average on social and psychological characteristics more frequently than their classmates. Another study compared boys whose fathers had been imprisoned and did not return permanently to the family with boys whose fathers were absent due to divorce (Moerk, 1973). Moerk found no significant differences between the two groups of boys on measures of the parent-child relationship, self-concept, or behavioral variables, though the sons of imprisoned fathers were more similar to juvenile delinquents than the boys from divorced families.

Sack (1977) and his colleagues (Sack, Seidler & Thomas, 1976) present clinical observations of children of imprisoned parents. A high percentage of children showed short-term behavioral symptoms soon after a parent was confined. The majority of these symptoms were mild disruptions, expressions of sadness, withdrawal, or a drop in school performance. Antisocial behavior of either a temporary or a more continuing type was observed in a small number of children. Sack et al. suggest that imprisonment functioned more as a precipitant than as a cause of antisocial behavior since it was only the most recent of a series of family crises for the children.

Incarceration is a separation that is often complicated by many other factors. In addition to the unlawful behavior that precipitated the arrest, conviction, and incarceration, there may be a history of illegal activities. The majority of female inmates are members of minority groups and come from low-status socioeconomic backgrounds. Many have not completed high school and typically have low job skills. Most female inmates are welfare recipients. In many cases, a convicted female is young, has high residential mobility, and is a mother in a single-parent situation (Skoler & McKeown, 1974). The profile of incarcerated women suggests that their families are disadvantaged and outside the mainstream of the community.

The moral stigma society generally attaches to incarceration creates a dimension of demoralization usually not present in other involuntary separations, except perhaps desertion and mental illness (Cappeller, 1972). A study exploring the attitudes of imprisoned mothers found they all had concerns about being away from their children, and the majority expressed some guilt about depriving their children of their care and about the children suffering for what they had done (Lundberg et al., 1975). This guilt may have produced fears on the mothers' part that the children would stop loving them and become more attached to their present caretakers. Depending on how a family views the situation, some are disgraced or demoralized by a parent's incarceration (Blackwell, 1959; Sack et al., 1976), others do not attach a moral connotation to the event. Feelings of shame and stigma were experienced almost exclusively by the wives of first-time offenders in the British study of prisoners' families (Morris, 1965). None of the wives of recidivists appeared to suffer from shame or stigma, though they expressed considerable anger at the way their children were treated by other children. In another study, about one-quarter of the wives of inmates reported that the children experienced some teasing by their peers (Sack et al. 1976). The stigma that members of the community attach to incarceration may detrimentally affect the social status and relations of a prisoner's family in the community. A criminal record is also a liability when seeking employment and, consequently, can jeopardize a family's economic circumstances.

A question arises about the role model a convicted mother presents to her child. Typically, a mother is thought of as an important role model and socializing agent for her child. Models who have high status and models who have been rewarding to a child are more likely to be imitated (Bandura & Walters, 1963). However, in studies by Bandura and Walters children who had imitated a baseball player discontinued their imitative behavior on learning the player was a convict. Does a convicted mother similarly lose respect and shift to a lower status in the eyes of her child?

It has been suggested that what happens to a model also influences the likelihood of imitation. Models who engage in disapproved activities without experiencing any adverse consequences are more likely to be imitated by children (Bandura & Walters, 1963; Soares & Soares, 1969). A child whose convicted mother is sentenced to probation rather than jail might see the mother as having "gotten away" with illegal conduct or at least having "gotten off" with a light punishment. In contrast, the child whose mother goes to jail has a vivid exposure to punishment and perhaps sees that "crime does not pay." Although these studies of deviant models have been primarily concerned with children's immediate responses to aggressive models, certainly similar processes might operate on a long-term basis. The possibility that a deviant parental model of behavior could contribute to a child's later antisocial conduct cannot be ruled out.

How does a child react to the mother as an authority figure after her conviction? Studies about children's compliance to mothers reveal conflicting results, depending on whether children's self-reports or behavior observations are used. While children report that the person who can make them obey is their mother (Tapp & Levine, 1970), observational studies show that children actually obey their own mothers much less than they do the mothers of other children (Landauer et al., 1970). In the present study mothers reported less obedience to their requests after incarceration, and older children considered their mothers to be less effective authority figures.

Previously little was known about the circumstances of children affected by parental imprisonment, either during the incarceration or afterward. Incarceration physically disrupts and also distorts the parent-child relationship. To untangle the effects of the incarceration from other complicating factors in the lives of convicted women, the imprisoned mothers were compared with mothers convicted of similar offenses but granted probation.

It was not known how a mother's conviction and incarceration were explained to a child or how a child reacts to such explanations. In a British study, Morris (1965) found 38 percent of over 400 families of male inmates had used partial or total deception in explanations given to children. Sack et al. (1976) found approximately one-third of the inmates' families practiced some form of deception in handling explanations to the children. The present study elicited information concerning the mother's explanation to the child as well as the child's version of what he was told and understood about his mother's absence.

Information was obtained about the mother-child relationship from both the mother and the child. A difficulty in this sort of questioning of mothers is the likelihood of inmates exaggerating their maternal solicitude. Women in jail may seek social approval from other inmates and staff by expressing concern about their children (Zalba, 1964; Zeitz, 1963). Social workers note that inmate mothers often express very unrealistic and idealized perceptions of their maternal role (Bonfanti et al., 1974) and of what life with their children will be like after they are released (Daehlin & Hynes, 1974). The Gluecks (1934) suggest that a period of imprisonment engenders an improved maternal attitude, based on their findings that 48 percent of the mothers were fond of and cared for their children during the postparole period, whereas only 14 percent did so before commitment. It would therefore be undesirable to base conclusions about maternal behavior solely on inmate self-reports. Questions about a mother's awareness of her child's activities, her contact with the child, and her disciplinary practices were also asked of the child in an attempt to verify the responses. Follow-up interviews at home revealed whether the mother and child are reunited and the conditions of the actual postrelease situation.

3 Legal Socialization

As legal competence becomes recognized as an important dimension of a person's general social skills, increased attention is being paid to the role of law in the socialization process of children. An objective of the socialization process is to produce individuals who will not only conform to the socially prescribed rules of conduct but will, as members of society, accept them as their own values (Maccoby, 1968). In legal socialization the goal is for individuals to learn to comply with the laws and accept designated authority in the law-making and law enforcement systems. In addition to conformity to the laws, it is desirable for children to acquire knowledge of laws and the consequences of breaking them, and develop the ability to make legal judgments based on notions of right and wrong.

Contemporary notions of how people learn to be law abiding have evolved from studies of the development of moral judgments and of ideas about law and legal authority (Piaget, 1932; Kohlberg, 1964; Hess & Torney, 1967; Tapp & Levine, 1970; Damon, 1977). Both cognitive developmental theory and social-learning theory contribute to an understanding of internalized moral values and behavior (Maccoby, 1968). Such moral development theorists as Piaget and Kohlberg are concerned with the cognitive aspects of moral growth and assume that a child's cognitive development provides a framework for and imposes restraints on the moral judgments a child is capable of at different ages. For example, the shift in a child's judgment from the view that rules and laws are absolute and unbreakable to the view that they are changeable and breakable is explained as cognitive maturation. Social-learning theorists treat the acquisition of moral behavior like other classes of behavior. The influence of training, modeling, and reinforcement by parents and other socializing agents also appears in a child's view of and involvement with the legal system.

The cognitive developmental view of moral growth as expounded by Kohlberg has strongly influenced legal socialization theory and research and has had an impact in the field of corrections. On the basis of his analysis of Piaget's findings and his own longitudinal and cross-cultural data, Kohlberg postulated three moral levels subdivided into six stages of moral development. There is good evidence from subjects' interview responses to hypothetical moral dilemmas that, when populations of children are considered as a whole, there is a developmental progression through his proposed sequence of moral-reasoning stages. Although Kohlberg's work shows there

13

is little relation between the content of what is judged right or wrong and actual moral behavior in natural or experimental settings, he maintains there are major differences in the form of moral orientation corresponding to developmental stages and that these differences in the form of judgment are related to actual moral behavior. Studies indicate differences between delinquents and nondelinquents in the form or stage of their moral orientation. Offenders are usually knowledgeable about society's laws, but most are at the lowest stages of moral development (Kohlberg & Freundlich, 1973).

This correspondence between an individual's stage of moral development and behavior has prompted some penal institutions to adopt Kohlberg's six-stage model of moral development in rehabilitation programs. The assumption is that rehabilitation goals can be achieved by promoting moral development. One approach to help individuals advance from one stage of moral reasoning to the next is to have discussions based on stories illustrating moral dilemmas. A more recent approach is the establishment of "just communities" in which participants engage in a process of self-government using moral discussion and democratic decision making. A living unit based on this moral development approach was established in a women's penal facility in Connecticut and the recidivism rate for participants was lowered (Kohlberg & Freundlich, 1973).

Other treatment programs for delinquents have been developed using a theory of personality and interpersonal maturity levels. The offenders are classified on the basis of their level of maturity and matched with compatible workers and treatment strategies in residential, community, or institutional settings. Studies indicate that differential treatments and settings may be useful in reducing the delinquent behavior of some juveniles (Palmer, 1974; Warren, 1969).

The compatibility of Kohlberg's moral development theory to concepts of law and legal justice is suggested by research on legal socialization (Tapp & Kohlberg, 1971). The link between cognitive moral development and the development of legal-reasoning capacity is stressed in Tapp's work on legal socialization. The legal-levels model that Tapp endorses is in part a variation and application of Kohlberg's moral levels to legal reasoning. Three levels of legal reasoning are postulated: (1) a preconventional law-obeying, punishment-oriented perspective; (2) a conventional law-and-order-maintaining, conformity-oriented perspective; and (3) a postconventional law-creating, principled perspective. National and cross-cultural surveys of children's opinions of law and justice have shown a predictable, age-related development in children's legal attitudes and an ordered progression from concrete notions to more abstract reasoning about law. The findings of other researchers are compatible with this model of legal-reasoning levels (Adelson et al., 1969; Adelson & Beall, 1970). The model was used as a framework for the analysis of children's legal reasoning in chapter 10 of this study.

Previous studies of legal reasoning have been normative in nature and have provided a reasonably comprehensive description of levels of legal reasoning by age group. However, they give no indication of how a child's individual experiences with the legal system and the police affect his legal perceptions. The present study compares the legal reasoning of children whose mothers are incarcerated with children whose mothers are on probation and the normative data describing children's legal reasoning.

The factor of personal experience may be especially important for the young child whose ability to engage in abstract reasoning about law and justice is limited. Hess and Torney (1967) suggest that children initially conceptualize about government and the legal system as persons to whom they can relate. Through "attachments" to these persons the child becomes oriented to the system. In this regard, a child's relationship with the police becomes a particularly appropriate topic for inquiry. The policeman is a salient figure and a personal representative of legal authority to the elementary school child (Greenstein, 1965; Hess & Torney, 1967). A child's interaction with the police may therefore be important in influencing his expectations concerning the more abstract system of law.

Most young children have high regard for the law and for law enforcement authorities (Hess & Torney, 1967). Studies show young children believe the job of police is to help persons in trouble and to prevent crimes, rather than to exercise the more punitive functions of catching and punishing criminals. They generally express a strong liking for the police, though this attraction declines steadily throughout elementary school years.

An unsuccessful effort was made in previous studies to determine what effect a child's contact with the police has on his attitudes toward them. They all conclude that adolescents who report police contact have less favorable attitudes toward the police than those who have no contact (Bouma, 1969; Portune, 1966) and delinquents are more hostile toward the police than nondelinquents (Chapman, 1956). The flaw in these studies is the problem of indeterminate causality. It could be that a child's attitude toward the police becomes less favorable after contact, but it is equally plausible that a child who already holds a low opinion of the police will engage in behavior that brings him to the attention of the police.

A similar problem exists with a study of adult criminal defendants who reported that they have never liked police, have always feared them, and have seen them as persons to be avoided (Casper, 1972). When asked about their first contact with the police, two-thirds spoke of personal encounters for law breaking when they were between the ages of 6 and 10. Although later events may color such recollections, it appears that the defendants' view of the police as adversaries had roots in their childhood experiences. Casper points out that even the social service functions of the police, such as assisting in the resolution of domestic disputes, may appear as unnecessary intrusions from a child's perspective and may contribute to the child's hostility toward the police.

4 Methodology

Design

To distinguish the effects of separation due to incarceration from the general effects of the mother's criminal involvement, children of incarcerated mothers are compared to children of mothers convicted of similar offenses but granted probation without any jail time.

Although it would have been desirable to interview the mothers and children before, during, and after the mother's incarceration, this was not practicable. The major problem was the impossibility of identifying ahead of time those children whose mothers would be incarcerated. Consequently, the best recourse was to contact the women after they had begun to serve their sentences and again after they were released.

The incarcerated mothers and their children were interviewed .twice, first while the mother was serving her sentence in the county jail (time I) and again about one month after she was released (time II). The person responsible for the care of a child during the mother's incarceration was also interviewed while the mother was imprisoned. The child's school was contacted for general achievement and behavior information for the periods before, during, and after the mother's incarceration.

The comparison group of mothers on probation and their children were also interviewed twice at intervals corresponding to those for incarcerated mothers and their children. The schools were contacted for similar information.

Subjects

The subjects were seventy-five mothers and their children who were between the ages of 4 and 18. Fifty-four mothers were incarcerated in county jails and twenty-one were on probation. The criteria for selecting the women were that they be sentenced and have a child over 4 years of age with whom they were living at the time of their arrest or when they turned themselves in. The anticipated release date of the incarcerated women had to fall within the projected duration of the study.

This study involved subjects from four California counties: Alameda, San Francisco, San Mateo, and Santa Clara. These Bay Area counties in-

17

clude urban areas (Oakland, San Francisco, and San Jose), a variety of racial and ethnic groups, and a complete socioeconomic range.

Procedure

The interviews of the incarcerated mothers and their children, as well as the caretakers and school personnel, were conducted by the investigator and a research assistant. Both are white, adult females. The interviews of mothers on probation, their children, and the school personnel were conducted by the investigator and two graduate research assistants, a white female and a Mexican-American, Spanish-speaking male. All the interviewers were trained by the investigator in interviewing techniques and conducted practice interviews before beginning to collect data for the study. The same person always conducted the first and second interviews for a given subject. It was believed that the positive practical effects of familiarity and rapport between the subject and interviewer outweighed the possible disadvantages of having the same person do both interviews.

The initial interview was conducted in jail for an incarcerated mother and at home for a mother on probation. For both groups, the second interview was conducted at the subject's residence. A child was seen wherever he was living at the time of the interviews.

The interviews were based on standard interview forms, but the questions were open-ended (Appendix A). An interview took approximately ten to twenty-five minutes for a child and forty-five to ninety minutes for a mother, depending on the number of children she had. The interviews were tape-recorded in most cases. If a person preferred not to be tape-recorded, the interviewer transcribed the responses by hand. All the interviews at the Santa Rita Jail in Alameda County were hand written because the sheriff did not allow tape recorders on the premises. Code numbers rather than names were used on tapes and transcripts.

The nature and purpose of the study were carefully explained to potential subjects (Appendix B). The interviewer explained that the study was not associated with the jail or probation department and that participation in the study could not improve or jeopardize an individual's status during or after incarceration or probation. It was stressed that any information given would be kept confidential. The sheriff in each of the four counties signed forms acknowledging the confidentiality of the information obtained in the interviews (Appendix C). All the subjects were told and reminded that they had the right to withdraw from the study, that they could discontinue the interview at any time, and that they could refuse to answer particular questions. Before an interview began the researcher answered any questions a subject had.

Participation by individuals in this study was strictly voluntary. Both written and oral consents were obtained from all subjects before an interview (Appendix D). Written consent was obtained from the mothers for permission to interview their minor children and permission was obtained from the child's current caretaker, if any, and any agency responsible for the care of the child.

Mothers were paid $25 for their participation in the study. The payment was made in cash after completion of the second interview. One function of the monetary compensation was to create an incentive for the women to complete the follow-up interview. It was felt that the compensation was reasonably related to the time spent in participation but was not so high as to constitute undue inducement.

The continuing policy of the investigator was to gather information from mothers and children as objectively as possible, without becoming a participant in their relationship by giving advice, acting as mediator, or relaying messages. The objective was to have as little impact on the participants' situation as possible. This study met the requirements of and was approved by the Stanford Committee on Human Subjects.

Participants on probation were obtained through the county adult probation departments. The study was thoroughly described to the probation officers who then informed mothers in their case loads about the research project. Women who were interested in participating in the study signed release forms to that effect (Appendix E). Their names were forwarded to the investigator who then contacted them. A descriptive record was kept of mothers on probation who chose not to participate.

The procedures for obtaining subjects in jail involved a number of steps. Initially, the study had to be cleared with county officials. After county approval, arrangements for the study had to be made with the director of each facility. The interviewers had to receive personal clearance from each of the four sheriffs for entry into the jails. The clearance procedure included fingerprinting, mug shots, and a background check. After obtaining clearance, the interviewer had general entry privileges into the jail (Appendix F).

Jail schedules restricted the time actually available for interviews to certain days and limited time periods. For each entry into the jail the interviewer's clearance status was checked, articles in her possession were frequently examined, and she was required to leave all items not necessary for the interview outside the custody area. Two of the facilities had security checks at the outside entrances of the jail grounds. All the jails checked the identity of individuals at the final entrance. Numerous situations arose that prevented the interviewer from entering a given jail where she had previously scheduled an interview. The primary reasons interviewers were denied entry were that the deputy in charge decided the jail was understaffed, too busy, or because there was a lockup. A lockup meant that the women were confined to their cells as a security measure, for punishment, or because the jail was understaffed.

When the interviewer obtained entry into a jail, she went through the files of women currently in custody to check for those who had been sentenced. Unsentenced women, including pretrial detainees, were not included in the study. Women whose expected release dates were within the projected duration of the study were considered potential subjects.

After determining that a woman was sentenced and that her expected release date was within the span of the study, the next step was to find out whether she had any children. Since the jails had no record of whether an inmate had children or other dependents, it was necessary to obtain this information from each woman personally. If a woman had a child over 4 years old with whom she had been living at the time of the arrest, she met the subject criteria for selection in the study.

The interview facilities varied from makeshift to adequate in the different jails. In no case was the interview setting pleasant or comfortable. In San Bruno, the San Francisco facility, there was no private interview space available. The interviewer was required to use the front entrance or a very small visitor section. This area barely accommodated two people and two chairs. In San Mateo County there was one small interview room available. If this room was being used by anyone else, such as an attorney or a probation officer, the interviewer could use the booking area, the day area, or a bunk in the woman's cell. At Santa Rita, in Alameda County, there was usually a room available for interviews. If this was occupied, the alternate interview space was in the pews of the jail chapel. At Elmwood, the Santa Clara facility, there were three designated interview rooms. These rooms were adequate for interviews, the only drawback being the constant background din caused by the ventilating system.

Although interviewing mothers in the jails had its discomforts and inconvenience, it was a fairly simple procedure compared to interviewing the children. Even though a mother in jail signed consent forms permitting her child to be interviewed, there was no guarantee her child could be seen. In some cases the mother did not know the address or phone number where her child was staying. Some of the children's residences did not have telephone service. A few children were never located. Occasionally, the child's current caretaker would not allow a child to be interviewed despite the mother's permission.

For children in foster care, the foster care agency was always contacted to obtain permission for the child's interview before the foster parents were contacted. This procedure caused some delay in one county where court approval was also required before seeing the children, but agency permission was then granted in all cases.

Typically, the interviewer arrived at the home before the child returned from school. To allow the child some time to become familiar with the interviewer, the interviewer carried a camera and took instantly produced color photos of the child. The camera often was a novelty for the children and readily prompted conversation. Children were allowed to keep all the photos that were taken. A few children requested extra photos to send to their mothers. After this period of familiarization each child was privately interviewed, if possible. In some instances the caretaker insisted on being present while the child was interviewed. The standard interview was modified for children who did not realize the mother was in jail. The questions that were omitted for these children are indicated on the interview form (Appendix A).

The school information was usually obtained from the child's teacher and, in some cases, from a counselor or the school principal. The interviewer did not disclose a mother's conviction and incarceration in those cases where school personnel were not aware of the situation. The information obtained from the schools at time I concerned the child's attendance record, academic performance measured by class rank, achievement tests, grades, and behavior at school. This information was collected for the periods before and during the mother's incarceration (Appendix G).

The interview of the mother on probation at time I was conducted in the home. It was scheduled in the afternoon before the child returned from school, and took thirty to forty-five minutes.

The child of a mother on probation was usually interviewed at home after he returned from school in the afternoon. The interviewer used the camera before the interview in the same manner as for children whose mothers were in jail. The standard interview was modified for children who did not realize that the mother was on probation. The questions that were omitted in these cases are marked on the interview form (Appendix A).

The school information for children of mothers on probation was obtained from the child's teacher, counselor, or school principal. The interviewer did not disclose a mother's conviction and probation in those cases where school personnel were not aware of the situation. The same school information form that was used for children of incarcerated mothers was used for children with mothers on probation (Appendix G).

The follow-up interviews at time II for both groups of mothers and children were conducted in the homes. The mother was interviewed first and paid $25 in cash upon completion of her interview. The interviewer had the camera again to take pictures for the child and the child was interviewed privately, if possible. In some cases the mother would insist on being present while her child was interviewed. The interviewer then requested that she remain silent and out of the child's line of vision. If the child had not been reunited with the mother at time II, the child and his current caretaker were interviewed where the child was living. The interviews at time II contained basically the same questions as at time I, except that the demographic and retrospective questions were not repeated and questions about the reunion and readjustment of mother and child were added.

Locating the mothers who had been in jail for the follow-up interview at time II was the most difficult task in the study. For a number of reasons it was frequently difficult, and sometimes impossible, to locate a woman after her release. In some cases women were in flight from further legal prosecution, reincarcerated in another part of the state, had changed residences leaving no forwarding address, or were using another name. A number of women were therefore untraceable.

Persistence was necessary to obtain interviews with many of the mothers because they repeatedly missed appointments for interviews in their homes. Patience in waiting until women returned home or rescheduling interviews was essential. One of the most effective strategies was to schedule the interview immediately upon contact with a mother, that is, within an hour of speaking to her on the telephone.

Obtaining information from the schools was another difficult and time-consuming process. School records were not easily accessible, even though written parental permission from the mother and current guardian was granted in all cases before seeking information from the schools. There was uneven access to school information about the children caused by different administrators' policies and a general absence of administrative procedures concerning research. Some school districts had elaborate research review arrangements to screen and discourage research in the schools; others were simply uncooperative.

Much of the inaccessibility was due to concerns of the school district administrators about privacy in student records. Other constraints were occasional arbitrary restrictions imposed by a principal or counselor. In one case a principal was unwilling to release information because he feared that it might be used by the mother in a divorce child-custody action against the father. The principal made it clear that he favored the father's efforts to obtain custody and strongly disapproved of the mother.

Several of the schools that willingly cooperated with the study had inadequate records about the children. In some instances teachers and counselors had been reluctant to make detailed written comments for the school records because they felt the files were not confidential. The fear was that written reports, especially those containing negative information, might be challenged someday by the child or parents in a lawsuit. Consequently, comments were typically nonevaluative. Several teachers were willing to discuss the children but would not make written reports. Inadequate school records were also caused by the recent enrollment of some children beginning school or older students who had transferred. In a few cases children had attended school so infrequently the schools did not have much information about them.

The findings of this study are presented in ten chapters. Chapters 5 and 6 describe the sample of mothers and children. Chapters 7 through 13 are concerned with hypothesis testing and presentation of the data, and are divided into two parts: analysis and discussion. Results are documented in the analysis, and selected findings are considered along with speculation about issues that arise in the discussion. Chapter 14 contains a brief summary of the major findings of the study and more discussion of policy issues. It describes programs for offenders with children and the Model Sentencing and Corrections Act, and concludes with suggestions for further research and recommendations.

Chi-square tests of statistical significance were used with the data in the tables. Chi-square is a method of determining whether variables are independent or whether a systematic relationship exists between them. A significant chi-square is interpreted as showing a relationship between the variables. The significance level of $p < .05$ was selected so that a result reported as statistically significant implies that a systematic relationship of some sort exists between the variables, with a chance of error 5 times out of 100, that is, a table with as large a deviation from the expected frequencies would occur by chance in only 5 samples out of 100. Results that are interpreted as not statistically significant at the $p < .05$ level are indicated by "N.S."

Percentages reported for the frequencies of observations are rounded to the nearest whole number, with .5 rounded up to even but not odd numbers. Consequently, the sum of percentages may be slightly more or less than 100 percent in some instances. Where subjects' responses were missing, they are omitted from tables unless otherwise noted, and thus column totals may occasionally be less than indicated.

In illustrative examples the names of mothers and children and other identifying features have in all cases been changed so identities of subjects are not disclosed.

5

Description of Mothers

Demographics

In the course of this study, seventy-five convicted female offenders were interviewed. All the women were mothers who had been living with their children at the time of arrest. Fifty-four were interviewed for the first time while they were serving sentences in county jails, and twenty-one while they were on probation. The mothers on probation had not been required to serve any jail time as a condition of probation. For definitional purposes, women in jail are referred to as "jail mothers" and women on probation as "probation mothers."

The majority of the women were under 30 years old and the jail mothers as a group were slightly younger. In fact, 37 percent of the jail mothers were less than 26 years old compared with 14 percent of the probation mothers (table 5-1*a*).

There was not a statistically significant difference in the racial distribution of these two groups. Approximately half of the women in each group were black, and the remainder were white, Mexican-American, native American, or of mixed racial ancestry (table 5-1*b*).

The marital histories of the two groups differed. With one exception, all the mothers on probation had been married at some time. In contrast, 35 percent of the jail mothers were single and had never been married (table 5-1*c*). At the time of arrest, 43 percent of the probation mothers and 30 percent of the jail mothers were married. In addition, 14 percent of the probation mothers and 17 percent of the jail mothers had common-law relationships at the time of arrest (table 5-1*d*).

There was no significant difference in the living arrangements of the women at the time of arrest; 37 percent of the jail mothers and 43 percent of the probation mothers lived with their children alone. An equal number of women lived with men, either a husband or in a common-law relationship (table 5-1*e*). Of those living with men, all the probation mothers' relationships exceeded one year in duration. One-fourth of the jail mothers who had been living with a man had lived with him for less than one year (table 5-1*f*). The remainder of the women lived with relatives or friends and their children.

There was not a significant difference in the women's recent residential mobility. More than half of both groups had lived in the same residence for

Table 5-1
Mothers' Demographics

	Jail Mothers (54)		Probation Mothers (21)		Significance
a. Age group					
18-25	37%	(20)	14%	(3)	N.S.
26-30	33	(18)	48	(10)	
31-35	17	(9)	14	(3)	
36-40	11	(6)	10	(2)	
41-50	2	(1)	14	(3)	
b. Racial group					
White	32%	(17)	48%	(10)	N.S.
Black	48	(26)	48	(10)	
Mexican-American	15	(8)	5	(1)	
Native American/other	5	(3)	—		
c. Martial history					
Never married	35%	(19)	5%	(1)	$p < .03$
Married once	50	(27)	71	(15)	
Married more than once	15	(8)	25	(5)	
d. Marital status					
Married	30%	(16)	43%	(9)	N.S.
Common-law relationship	17	(9)	14	(3)	
Single	20	(11)	5	(1)	
Separated/divorced/widowed	33	(18)	38	(8)	
e. Living arrangement					
Children alone	37%	(20)	43%	(9)	N.S.
Husband and children	17	(9)	33	(7)	
Common law and children	20	(11)	10	(2)	
Parents and children	11	(6)	5	(1)	
Others and children	15	(8)	10	(2)	
f. Duration living with man					
Less than 1 year	9%	(5)	—		$p < .05$
More than 1 year	28	(15)	57%	(12)	
Does not apply	63	(34)	43	(9)	
g. Length of residence					
Less than 1 year	44%	(24)	38%	(8)	N.S.
Longer than 1 year	56	(30)	62	(13)	
h. Residential mobility in last 3 years					
No moves	31%	(16)	24%	(5)	N.S.
1-3 moves	42	(22)	62	(13)	
4 or more moves	27	(14)	14	(3)	
i. Socioeconomic status (Hollingshead index)					
Level II-III	8%	(4)	5%	(1)	$p < .01$
Level IV	13	(7)	48	(10)	
Level V (lowest)	80	(43)	48	(10)	

Table 5-1 *(continued)*

	Jail Mothers (54)	Probation Mothers (21)	Significance
j. Employment			
Unemployed	65%(35)	38% (8)	p < .01
Low or unskilled	20 (11)	10 (2)	
Skilled, sales, clerical, etc.	15 (8)	52 (11)	
k. Receiving welfare			
Yes	68%(37)	81%(17)	N.S.
No	32 (17)	19 (4)	
l. Occupational classification for female offenders[1]			
Professional	—	5% (1)	p < .03
Managers	4% (2)	—	
Semiprofessional technicians	4 (2)	19 (4)	
Skilled workers, craftsmen	—	5 (1)	
Clerical workers	4 (2)	19 (4)	
Sales workers	4 (2)	5 (1)	
Semiskilled workers	7 (4)	5 (1)	
Personal services	6 (3)	5 (1)	
Unskilled workers	7 (4)	—	
Unemployed	65 (35)	38 (8)	
m. Education			
Some college	17% (9)	43% (9)	p < .05
High school graduate	26 (14)	24 (5)	
Some high school	39 (21)	33 (7)	
9th grade or less	18 (10)	—	

Chi-square (χ^2) tests of statistical significance are used in all tables. N.S. indicates that χ^2 was not significant at the .05 level.

[1]R.M. Glick and V.V. Neto, *National Study of Women's Correctional Programs*, Washington, D.C.: National Institute of Law Enforcement and Criminal Justice, 1977.

longer than one year (table 5-1*g*). Approximately one-fourth of the jail mothers had moved four or more times in the past three years (table 5-1*h*).

The majority of both groups were in the lowest socioeconomic levels according to the Hollingshead two factor index of social position (Hollingshead, 1957). However, there were significantly more jail mothers (80 percent) in the bottom category. The probation mothers were almost equally divided between the two lowest categories (table 5-1*i*).

There was a statistically significant difference in the employment status of the two groups at the time of arrest. Sixty-five percent of the jail mothers were unemployed at that time, whereas 62 percent of the probation mothers had jobs (table 5-1*j*). Some mothers, particularly those on probation, had been working and receiving welfare assistance at the same time. A majority of both groups were receiving some kind of public financial support, typically

Aid to Families with Dependent Children (table 5-1*k*). If income is low enough, one can legally qualify for welfare support. It should also be noted that a number of the women, particularly those on probation, had been convicted of welfare fraud, often for not reporting all sources of income.

It became apparent that the Hollingshead two factor index of social position was not well suited for the sample of women in the study. Some of the conventional jobs they held, such as child-care worker, were not included in Hollingshead's job breakdown. Needless to say, such nonconventional jobs as stripper, prostitute, or heroin dealer were not included either. Therefore another occupation classification developed specifically for female offenders was also used (Glick & Neto, 1977; Appendix H). Whereas in the Hollingshead scale the women were primarily in the lowest two categories, the classification for female offenders displays more diversity in the women's occupational roles (table 5-1*l*).

There was a significant difference in the educational backgrounds of the women. More than half of the jail mothers had not completed high school, compared to one-third of the probation mothers. Eighteen percent of the jail mothers had only a ninth-grade education or less, while none of the probation mothers were in this category. In contrast, 43 percent of the probation mothers had had some college experience, compared to 17 percent of the jail mothers (table 5-1*m*).

Criminal Involvement of Mothers

There was not a significant difference in the general categories of offenses committed by the two groups of mothers, though there were differences within the general categories of violent, property, and narcotics offenses (table 5-2*a*).

Many of the women were serving time concurrently on a number of charges. In that event, all the offenses for which a woman was serving time were recorded (table 5-2*b*) but she was categorized according to the crime for which she had received the longest sentence (table 5-2*a*). That is, if a woman were sentenced to nine months for petty theft and ninety days for possession of narcotics, she was categorized as a property offender.

The majority of the women were categorized as property offenders. The jail mothers' property offenses included both petty and grand theft, in addition to forgery, embezzlement, credit card offenses, and welfare fraud. However, property offenses for the probation mothers were mostly welfare fraud and forgery. The violent crimes included drunk driving and armed robbery for both groups, plus burglary, assault, and manslaughter for women in jail (table 5-2*b*).

It should be recognized that plea bargaining plays an important role in the judicial process. Plea bargaining is the pretrial process by which the prosecutor and the defense attorney negotiate a disposition of the defendant's case without a trial. That disposition may involve a plea of guilty to a less serious offense than was originally charged or an agreement on the sentence that will be recommended to the court. For example, a woman arrested for selling heroin may agree to plead guilty to a lesser charge of possession of heroin instead of going to trial on the original charge and thereby minimize the risk of a harsher sentence if she were found guilty after a trial.

Although narcotics offenses account for only one-quarter of the convictions, drug use is an important factor to consider in interpreting the offense data. Drugs were often indirectly involved in the other offense categories. For example, a woman convicted of petty theft may acknowledge that her motive was to obtain funds to support her heroin addiction. Such admissions among the property offenders were not unusual.

Drug use among women in this study was quite common and the need for money to buy narcotics was cited as a motivation for some of the crimes. Half of the jail mothers acknowledged heavy drug usage and two-thirds of this group admitted they were addicted. An additional 15 percent of the jail mothers considered themselves alcoholics and another 6 percent admitted to both drug and alcohol problems. In contrast, the use of drugs and alcohol was not as prevalent among the probation mothers. Only 20 percent acknowledged extensive drug use and half of that group admitted addiction. Another 10 percent considered themselves alcoholics and 5 percent reported both drug and alcohol problems (table 5-2c). The habitual use of drugs and alcohol was characteristic of 70 percent of the jail mothers and 35 percent of the probation mothers. Many of these women lived in communities in which drug traffic was relatively common. Occasional or casual use of alcohol, marijuana, and other similar drugs was not defined as an alcohol problem or as drug use in this study.

A review of the histories of these women reveals a long-standing pattern of criminal exposure, dating back to childhood for some. This pattern of criminal exposure was substantially greater for the jail mothers. Beginning with the women's primary families, the pattern clearly emerges and differentiates the jail group from the probation group. Over half of the jail mothers came from families in which a family member (parent, sibling, or several family members) had also spent time in jail or prison. This is not so to the same extent for the probation mothers' families, where only 14 percent had a family member who had served time in a penal institution (table 5-2d).

Despite the difference in family backgrounds, a sharp difference between the jail and probation mothers' experience in the justice system does not begin to emerge until early adulthood. Juvenile delinquency records reveal no significant difference between these two groups concerning the likelihood of contact with the juvenile court, though more jail mothers had juvenile records and a slightly higher percentage had spent time in juvenile correctional institutions (table 5-2e). No distinguishing prediction of the

Table 5-2
Mothers' Criminal Involvement

	Jail Mothers (54)		Probation Mothers (21)		Significance
a. Offense categories					
Property	50%	(27)	62%	(13)	N.S.
Violent	22	(12)	14	(3)	
Narcotics	26	(14)	24	(5)	
Other	2	(1)	—		
b. Offenses					
Manslaughter	3%	(2)	—		N.S.
Robbery, attempted robbery	3	(2)	4%	(1)	
Assault, assault with deadly weapon	5	(4)	—		
Burglary	4	(3)	—		
Drunk driving	4	(3)	9	(2)	
Forgery/fraud/credit cards/ embezzlement	23	(17)	18	(4)	
Larceny-theft, grand auto theft	11	(8)	9	(2)	
Welfare fraud	7	(5)	45	(10)	
Narcotics	25	(18)	14	(3)	
Contributing to delinquency of minor	1	(1)	—		
Extortion, conspiracy	3	(2)	—		
Concealed weapon	3	(2)	—		
Perjury	4	(3)	—		
Prostitution	3	(2)	—		
Suspended license	1	(1)	—		
c. Drug use					
Nonuser	30%	(16)	65%	(13)	N.S.
Drug use	17	(9)	10	(2)	
Drug addict	33	(18)	10	(2)	
Alcoholic	15	(8)	10	(2)	
Durg and alcohol problem	6	(3)	5	(1)	
d. Family member incarceration					
No	46%	(25)	86%	(18)	$p < .01$
Parents	9	(5)	—		
Several members (siblings, parents)	44	(24)	14	(3)	
e. Juvenile delinquency record					
No	59%	(32)	76%	(16)	N.S.
Yes	20	(11)	10	(2)	
Yes and time served	18	(10)	14	(3)	
f. Age at first arrest					
20 or less	32%	(17)	19%	(4)	N.S.
21-25	26	(14)	33	(7)	
26-30	22	(12)	24	(5)	
31-35	15	(8)	19	(4)	
36-40	4	(2)	—		
41-50	2	(1)	5	(1)	

Table 5-2 *(continued)*

	Jail Mothers (54)	Probation Mothers (21)	Significance
g. Prior adult arrest			
No	41%(22)	71%(15)	$p < .03$
Yes	59 (32)	29 (6)	
h. Prior probation			
No	48%(26)	71%(15)	$p < .01$
Yes	4 (2)	24 (5)	
Yes, current violations	28 (15)	5 (1)	
Yes, prior violations	11 (6)	—	
Yes, current and prior violations	9 (5)	—	
i. Prior adult incarceration			
No	52%(28)	81%(17)	$p < .05$
1-2 times	30 (16)	19 (4)	
3+ times	19 (10)	—	
j. Friends' criminal incarceration			
No	32%(17)	62%(13)	$p < .05$
Yes	59 (32)	38 (8)	
No friends	9 (5)	—	
k. Arrested/turned self in			
Turned self in	11% (6)	43% (9)	$p < .01$
Arrested	89 (48)	57 (12)	
l. Detained			
No	13% (7)	50%(10)	$p < .01$
Yes	87 (46)	50 (10)	

Chi-square (χ^2) tests of statistical significance are used in all tables. N.S. indicates that χ^2 was not significant at the .05 level.

women's adult criminal involvement could be made from the juvenile records. The fact that there was no significant difference in the women's ages at the time of their first adult arrest also suggests a similarity in their early personal experiences with the legal system (table 5-2*f*).

It was upon arrival in adult court that a difference began to emerge. Fifty-nine percent of the jail mothers had prior arrests compared to 29 percent of the probation mothers (table 5-2*g*). Slightly over half of the jail mothers had prior experience on probation and of those, all but two had had either a past or current probation violation. Twenty-nine percent of the probation mothers had previously been on probation but only one had a current violation (table 5-2*h*). Similarly, 49 percent of the jail mothers had experienced a previous adult incarceration compared to 19 percent of the probation mothers (table 5-2*i*).

Over half of the jail mothers reported having friends outside jail who had previously served time, compared to 38 percent of the probation mothers. A few jail mothers reported having no friends at all (table 5-2*j*).

The current status of these two groups displayed a growing disparity in their criminal histories. There was a significant statistical difference between the groups as to whether they had been arrested or had surrendered themselves to the authorities for the current offense. Eighty-nine percent of the jail mothers were arrested and 11 percent turned themselves in to the police. The situation was different for the probation group where 57 percent were arrested but 43 percent had turned themselves in (table 5-2*k*). An impending warrant for arrest was often the instigating factor prompting a woman to surrender herself.

Treatment of the two groups at the time of arrest or self-surrender differed significantly: 87 percent of the jail mothers were detained compared to only 50 percent of the probation mothers (table 5-2*l*). A high percentage of the women arrested were detained whereas women who surrendered themselves were unlikely to be held in custody at that time.

Legal Situation of Mothers

Most of the women in both groups were represented in their recent legal proceedings by public defenders because they could not afford to retain private attorneys (table 5-3*a*). The one probation mother who did not have

Table 5-3
Mothers' Legal Situation

	Jail Mothers[1] (20)	Probation Mothers (21)	Significance
a. Legal counsel			
Public defender	75%(15)	86%(18)	N.S.
Private attorney	25 (5)	10 (2)	
No	—	5 (1)	
b. Satisfied with lawyer			
Yes	70%(14)	48%(10)	N.S.
No	10 (2)	33 (7)	
Does not know	20 (4)	14 (3)	
Does not apply	—	5 (1)	
c. Want same lawyer again			
Yes	50%(10)	33% (7)	N.S.
No	25 (5)	38 (8)	
Does not know	15 (3)	19 (4)	
Does not apply	—	5 (1)	
Not codable	10 (2)	5 (1)	

Table 5-3 *(continued)*

	Jail Mothers[1] (20)	Probation Mothers (21)	Significance
d. Plea bargain			
Yes	75% (15)	62% (13)	N.S.
No	25 (5)	14 (3)	
Does not know	—	24 (5)	
e. Opinion about plea bargain			
Positive	30% (6)	10% (2)	$p < .05$
Negative, unfair	15 (3)	28 (6)	
Usual procedure, not positive			
or negative	25 (5)	5 (1)	
No opinion	5 (1)	38 (8)	
Does not apply	25 (5)	19 (4)	
f. Opinion about sentencing judge			
Neutral	55% (11)	24% (5)	N.S.
Concerned about mother	20 (4)	52 (11)	
Hostile, against mother	20 (4)	24 (5)	
Does not know, no opinion	5 (1)	—	
g. Opinion about sentence			
Fair	55% (11)	57% (12)	N.S.
Unfair, too harsh	20 (4)	38 (8)	
Does not know, uncertain	25 (5)	5 (1)	
h. Explanation of sentence			
Prior criminal record	45% (9)	—	$p < .001$
Offense itself, mandatory	20 (4)	—	
Harsh sentence, political	15 (3)	—	
Plea bargained	10 (2)	10% (2)	
Lenient sentence, political	—	5 (1)	
First offense, no record	—	24 (5)	
Mother with children	—	43 (9)	
Does not know, no opinion	10 (2)	19 (4)	

Chi-square (χ^2) tests of statistical significance are used in all tables. N.S. indicates that χ^2 was not significant at the .05 level.

[1]Questions concerning a mother's legal situation were asked in the follow-up interview at time II. Consequently the number of jail mothers responding is reduced.

legal counsel said she did not think she needed an attorney. The jail mothers expressed greater satisfaction with their attorneys than the probation mothers (table 5-3b). They also were more likely to want the same lawyer again if the need for legal assistance arose in the future (table 5-3c).

All but one of the women pled guilty to charges rather than go to trial. The majority of the women's cases involved some plea bargaining (table 5-3d). Given the prevalent reliance on plea bargaining as a means of handling criminal cases in the American legal system, it is not surprising that none of the women in the study had a jury trial. According to Chief Justice

Warren Burger in an address to the American Bar Association (1970), only 10 percent of persons charged with a criminal offense have trials; the other 90 percent plead guilty.

Over one-fifth of the probation mothers were unsure whether there had been any plea bargaining in their cases; this is probably a reflection of their relative inexperience with the routine plea negotiations that occur between prosecutors and defense attorneys.

The jail mothers expressed more understanding and acceptance of the plea-bargaining process as a standard procedure than the probation mothers. Although presumably some of the probation mothers avoided jail sentences by means of plea bargaining, 28 percent felt plea bargaining had been disadvantageous for them (table 5-3e). While no one complained about overly strict conditions of probation, some had probation with a suspended jail sentence. In those cases, the threat existed of revocation of probation and imprisonment if they committed any new offenses or violated a condition of probation.

The fairness and compassion of the sentencing judge were viewed differently by the two groups of women. More than half of the jail mothers who expressed opinions on this matter felt the judge was neutral and fair. The other jail mothers were split in thinking the judge was either concerned about their welfare or was hostile toward them. Approximately half of the probation mothers felt the judge showed compassion and was concerned for their welfare, with the others split in thinking the judge was either hostile or neutral (table 5-3f). When asked whether they felt the judge had been fair or unfair in the sentencing, the majority of both groups considered the judge to have acted fairly and felt the sentence they received was fair (table 5-3g).

When mothers were asked why they felt the judge gave them the particular sentence of jail time or probation, responses varied significantly. The most common explanation by almost half of the jail mothers was that they received the sentence because of prior criminal records or they were already on probation. The second most common answer of the jail mothers was that the offense they committed either had a mandatory sentence or involved a large amount of money. Another 15 percent attributed their jail sentence to the generally harsh sentences given by particular judges and to the political considerations of an upcoming judicial election (table 5-3h).

In contrast, the most common explanation given by the probation mothers for their getting probation without any jail time was that they were mothers with young children. Although having children may have been an influential factor in individual cases, it clearly was not a decisive factor for everyone. The next most frequent response was that they had no prior adult criminal record or had generally good conduct.

6 Description of Children

Demographics

The 75 mothers in this study had a total of 166 children about whom information was gathered. This discussion is based on information about these children obtained from interviews with all the mothers, interviews with 49 children of mothers in jail, and interviews with 35 children of mothers on probation. For definitional purposes, children of mothers in jail are referred to as "jail" children and children of mothers on probation as "probation" children.

Several factors contributed to the reduced number of children who were interviewed. Although all the mothers participating in the study granted permission for their children to be interviewed and signed permission forms, a mother's grant of permission was no guarantee of accessibility to her children. For instance, court authorization was required before it was possible to interview children in foster care. In other cases, temporary guardians refused permission for children's interviews. In a few cases, children could not be located and several teen-aged boys refused to cooperate.

There was a difference in the racial distribution of the two groups of children who were interviewed: 73 percent of the jail children were black compared with 46 percent of the probation children. Only 17 percent of the jail children were white compared to 51 percent of the probation children. The remaining children were of Mexican-American descent (table 6-1a). There was not a corresponding difference in the racial distribution of the mothers. Several factors account for this disparity. The children's interviews that were completed included a disproportionately large number of black jail children and a small number of white jail children. This in part reflects a differential success rate in obtaining interviews with the jail children and the fact that black mothers had slightly larger families. In addition, one jail mother who was classified white and two jail mothers who classified themselves as "other" for ethnic group because of mixed racial ancestry, had children who were listed as black.

In the areas of age, sex, grade in school, and number of siblings, no statistically significant differences were evident between jail and probation children who were interviewed (table 6-1b, c, d, and e).

The children ranged in age from 4 to 18. Most of the children were less than 14 years old and attended elementary or junior high school. Seven of

Table 6-1
Children's Demographics

	Jail Children (49)	Probation Children (35)	Significance
a. Racial group			
White	17% (8)	51%(18)	$p<.003$
Black	73 (35)	46 (16)	
Mexican-American	10 (5)	3 (1)	
b. Age			
4-8	47%(23)	40%(14)	N.S.
9-13	33 (16)	54 (19)	
14-18	20 (10)	6 (2)	
c. Sex			
Boy	55%(27)	43%(15)	N.S.
Girl	45 (22)	57 (20)	
d. Grade in school			
K or 1st	18% (8)	23% (8)	N.S.
2d	20 (9)	11 (4)	
3d	7 (3)	9 (3)	
4th	9 (4)	17 (6)	
5th	7 (3)	9 (3)	
6th	4 (2)	17 (6)	
7th	7 (3)	6 (2)	
8th	2 (1)	6 (2)	
9th or higher	11 (5)	3 (1)	
Not in school	16 (7)		
e. Number of siblings			
None	10% (4)	14% (5)	N.S.
1 or 2	56 (22)	37 (13)	
3 or 4	18 (7)	31 (11)	
5 or more	16 (6)	17 (6)	

	Jail Children (118)	Probation Children (48)	Significance
f. Source of financial support before mother's sentence			
Mother alone	8%(10)	4% (2)	N.S.
Welfare, Aid to Dependent Children	76 (90)	83 (40)	
Other source	14 (17)	12 (6)	
Grandparents	1 (1)	—	

Chi-square (χ^2) tests of statistical significance are used in all tables. N.S. indicates that χ^2 was not significant at the .05 level.

the children in the jail group were not currently in school, either because they had dropped out of high school or had started kindergarten or first grade but did not attend class regularly enough to be considered currently enrolled by the schools (table 6-1*d*).

The size of the families ranged from one child to eight children (table

6-1*e*). Sex distribution was approximately equal within and between groups (table 6-1*c*).

Based on information from the mothers' interviews, there was not a significant difference in the children's source of financial support at the time of the mother's arrest. Most of the children in both groups were receiving Aid to Families with Dependent Children (AFDC). Some were supported by the mothers and others, and a minority by mothers alone (table 6-1*f*).

Social Situation of Child

As expected, children whose mothers were sentenced to jail were subjected to more disruptions in their lives. Within the scope of the study, this pattern begins at the time of the mother's arrest and continues throughout the course of the study.

What most immediately affects the child at the time of the mother's arrest is whether or not she is detained. Detention can range from overnight to several weeks, often depending on what amount of bail is set. If the mother is detained, as 87 percent of the women who were eventually jailed were, the child experiences an abrupt loss of the mother. This situation was experienced by 78 percent of the jail and 43 percent of the probation children (table 6-2*a*).

An effort was made to determine whether or not the mother expressed concern about the well-being and whereabouts of her children at the time of her arrest and possible detention. Mothers were asked if they had used one of their legally permitted phone calls at that time to inquire about or make arrangements for the care of their children. Approximately two-thirds of both groups of mothers reported that they made an effort to do this. Of course, mothers who surrendered themselves and those who anticipated arrest because of outstanding warrants were in a position to make prior arrangements for the children's care (table 6-2*b*).

During the interim while the mothers were initially detained, 38 percent of the jail and 15 percent of the probation children experienced one or more changes in their living situations (table 6-2*c*). Arrangements during this time had to be made swiftly and without knowledge of how long the mother would be absent.

When the women were sentenced, they divided into the two groups of jail and probation mothers. In all cases, the mothers on probation were permitted to remain at home with their children. For the women sentenced to jail, arrangements had to be made for the care of their children for the duration of their jail terms, which ranged from one month to thirteen months with potential for earlier release based on "good time."

Half of the jail children were not consulted about where they would stay

Table 6-2
Children's Living Situation

	Jail Children (118)	Probation Children (48)	Significance
a. Mother detained at time of arrest			
Yes	78%(91)	43%(20)	$p<.001$
No	22 (25)	57 (27)	
b. Mother's concern about child's well-being at arrest/detention			
Yes	69%(81)	62%(30)	$p<.001$
No	20 (23)	—	
Does not apply	12 (14)	38 (18)	
c. Changes in child's living arrangement during detention			
No change	40%(47)	29%(14)	$p<.001$
Some changes	38 (45)	15 (7)	
Does not apply	21 (25)	56 (27)	
d. Jail child consulted about arrangements			
No	50%(59		
Yes, approved	32 (38)		
Yes, not approved	11 (13)		
Missing	7 (8)		
e. Child's living arrangement during mother's sentence (time 1)			
Grandparent	35%(41)	—	$p<.001$
"Father"	22 (26)	—	
Other relative	20 (23)	—	
Foster care	10 (12)	—	
Sibling/self	8 (9)	—	
Other	6 (7)	2% (1)	
Mother	—	40 (19)	
Mother and "father"	—	44 (21)	
Mother and grandparent	—	6 (3)	
Mother and other	—	8 (4)	
f. Changes in child's care taking arrangement during mother's sentence			
No, single arrangement	62%(73)	98%(47)	$p<.001$
Yes, several	38 (45)	2 (1)	
g. Siblings separated during mother's sentence			
No	55%(65)	88%(42)	$p<.001$
Yes	25 (29)	2 (1)	
Does not apply	20 (24)	10 (5)	

Table 6-2 *(continued)*

	Jail Children *(118)*	Probation Children *(48)*	Significance
h. Child changed schools after mother's arrest or during sentence			
No	42%(50)	65%(31)	*p*<.005
Yes	42 (50)	15 (7)	
Does not apply	15 (18)	21 (10)	
i. Child's source of financial support before mother's sentence (time 0)			
Mother alone	8%(10)	4% (2)	N.S.
Welfare	76 (90)	83 (40)	
Other source	14 (17)	12 (6)	
Grandparents	1 (1)	—	
j. Child's source of financial support during mother's sentence (time 1)			
Mother alone	—	6% (3)	*p*<.01
Welfare	72%(85)	73 (35)	
Other source	18 (21)	15 (7)	
Grandparents	10 (12)	—	

Chi-square (χ^2) tests of statistical significance are used in all tables. N.S. indicates that χ^2 was not significant at the .05 level.

during their mother's absence. Approximately one-third approved of their new situations, but 11 percent expressed dissatisfaction or opposition to the arrangements that had been made for them (table 6-2*d*).

After the jail mothers began serving their sentences, their children usually had a living arrangement that was different from the situation before the mother's arrest, but it was often a continuation of the arrangement that existed during the mother's detention. During their mothers' incarceration 35 percent of the jail children lived with grandparents, usually the maternal grandmother; 22 percent with fathers or a male companion of the mother; 20 percent with other relatives; 10 percent in foster care; 8 percent on their own or with an older sibling; and 6 percent in some other arrangement, such as with neighbors or friends of the mother (table 6-2*e*). Living arrangements for 62 percent of the jail children endured for the length of the mother's sentence, while the other 38 percent had one or more changes from the initial placement (table 6-2*f*).

Separation from siblings was one of the most serious changes experienced. Of the ninety-four jail children who had siblings, 31 percent were separated from each other during their mother's incarceration (table 6-2g).

Significantly more jail than probation children changed schools while their mothers were serving sentences. That is, 42 percent of the jail children, or half of those who attended school at the time, compared to only 15 percent of the probation children had changed schools (table 6-2h). Typically a change of schools was the consequence of a change in residence.

Another potential change in the life of a child of an incarcerated mother is the source and perhaps level of financial support. Before the incarceration, 76 percent of the jail children were supported by welfare, 14 percent by some other source, 8 percent by the mother alone, and 1 percent by a grandparent. During the mother's incarceration there was a shift in financial support for some children. The number receiving AFDC declined to 72 percent and those receiving support from others increased to 18 percent (table 6-2i and j). None of the jail mothers continued to provide the primary financial support for her children. A more complete analysis and discussion of the children's financial support is included in chapter 12.

7 Mother's Knowledge of Child

Analysis

Expressing concern about one's children is a highly condoned activity in women's correctional institutions. This fact could result in conscious or unconscious distortions by inmate mothers as to the adequacy of the care they gave their children before they were incarcerated (Zalba, 1964). It could also contribute to the mothers' often unrealistic plans for their children's care after release (Martin & Webster, 1971). Inmate mothers may idealize themselves in their maternal roles to compensate for the derogation they experience by being cast in the role of criminals (Bonfanti et al., 1974). It was hypothesized that jail mothers would have less knowledge than probation mothers concerning their children's activities and interests. Since a mother's failure to express concern about her children could result in social ostracism within the jail, factual questions that could be verified were used as a measure of the mother's actual awareness of and concern for her children's situation.

It is not surprising that a mother's day-to-day knowledge of her children would diminish while she was in jail. What is surprising is that there was a discernible difference between the jail and probation mothers in their knowledge of matters that predated the sentencing and would remain relatively unchanged by incarceration. The topics queried dealt with ongoing kinds of information relating to the child's school attendance and acquaintances. Despite the fact that incarceration should not have a substantial bearing on this kind of knowledge, the jail mothers revealed a very low level of awareness of their children's activities.

A mother's incarceration would not be an adequate explanation for her not knowing certain kinds of information, such as the age of her child. In fact, most mothers could report children's ages—occasionally with some hesitation—within a year or so.

However, when areas of activities and interests were examined, jail mothers had less knowledge than probation mothers. Since almost all the children in the study were of school age, school-related questions were appropriate. The mothers were asked the following four questions:

1. Did your child stay in the same school or did he change schools since the time of your arrest?

2. What is the name of the school your child attends?
3. What grade is your child in?
4. What is the name of your child's teacher?

To get an overall impression of how well informed the mothers were about their children's school situation, a scale was developed on the basis of their ability to answer these four school-related questions. Only 4 percent of the jail children's mothers could answer all four questions, compared to 44 percent in the probation group. Some of the jail mothers' knowledge was so scanty that for one-third of the jail children, the mothers could answer only one or none of the items, compared to only 4 percent in the probation group (table 7-1a).

When the mothers were asked "did your child stay in the same school or

Table 7-1
Mothers' Knowledge of Child's School Information and Friends

	Jail Mothers by Child (118)	Probation Mothers by Child (48)	Significance
a. Mother's summed knowledge of school information			
Answered none *or* 1 question	34%(40)	4% (2)	$p<.001$
Answered 2-3 questions	42 (50)	35 (17)	
Answered all 4 questions	4 (5)	44 (21)	
Does not apply	9 (11)	4 (2)	
Missing, not codable	10 (12)	12 (6)	
b. Mother's report whether child changed schools since her arrest			
Yes, change	42%(50)	15% (7)	$p<.001$
No change	42 (50)	65 (31)	
Does not know	10 (12)	—	
Missing	5 (6)	21 (10)	
c. Mother's report of child's grade in school			
K-1	15%(18)	8% (4)	$p<.03$
2	10 (12)	6 (3)	
3	8 (9)	10 (5)	
4	3 (4)	10 (5)	
5-6	7 (8)	23 (11)	
7-8	5 (6)	6 (3)	
9 or higher	12 (14)	10 (5)	
Not in school	12 (14)	6 (3)	
Does not know	14 (16)	—	
Missing	14 (17)	19 (9)	

Table 7-1 *(continued)*

	Jail Children (118)	Probation Children (48)	Significance
d. Mother's report on seeing child's report card			
Yes	66%(78)	88%(42)	$p<.03$
Sometimes	5 (6)	—	
No	8 (9)	—	
Does not apply	14 (16)	4 (2)	
Missing	8 (9)	8 (4)	
e. Mother's knowledge of child's friends			
None	58%(68)	33%(16)	$p<.005$
One	23 (27)	27 (13)	
Knows	10 (12)	31 (15)	
Missing	9 (11)	8 (4)	

	Jail Children (38)	Probation Children (32)	Significance
f. Child's report whether mother sees report card			
Yes	82%(31)	78%(25)	N.S.
No	18 (7)	22 (7)	
g. Child's report whether mother knows friends			
Yes	92%(33)	83%(25)	N.S.
No	6 (2)	17 (5)	
Does not apply	3 (1)	—	

Chi-square (χ^2) tests of statistical significance are used in all tables. N.S. indicates that χ^2 was not significant at the .05 level.

did he change schools since the time of your arrest?'' there was no difference between the groups in the mothers' ability to answer. Most of the mothers knew whether or not their child had changed schools. There was a noticeably higher number of jail children who had changed schools, which was usually accounted for by the child's change of residence (table 7-1*b*).

When asked ''what is the name of the school your child attends?'' many mothers, particularly jail mothers, were unable to name the specific school in which their child was currently enrolled. They could usually specify whether it was public or parochial and often gave the approximate location. A few asked for more time to think about the answer.

When asked ''what grade is your child in?'' all probation mothers could answer. But 14 percent of the jail mothers did not know their child's grade level. Interviewers reported that the mothers' answers were more uncertain when the children were in junior or senior high school (table 7-1*c*).

When asked "what is the name of your child's teacher?" many mothers were at a loss for an answer. This proved to be the most difficult question. This difficulty was more understandable when the children were in high school and had several teachers, though a single correct name was recorded as a correct response. Some mothers laughed in response to this question and expressed the attitude that you could not expect them to know everything.

Interviewers reported some surprise at the nonchalance with which some jail mothers accepted their inability to answer three out of the four questions. Some mothers expressed the opinion that these kinds of questions were more appropriately asked of the children. More often, jail mothers who failed to answer the questions would offer some excuse such as "the information changes so often I can't keep track," "it's just slipped my mind," or "I don't get to school to see the teacher and find out."

Perhaps school and school-related information had less importance to these women than middle-class Americans assign them. The jail mothers themselves had poor academic records, with more than half not having graduated from high school. Although interest in their children's school achievement might have been lower than average, this explanation appeared unlikely. Later in the interview and in conversation, most of the mothers expressed the commonly held belief that it was important for their children to do well and to go as far as they could in school.

Not unexpectedly, given the lack of information about school the mothers displayed, 13 percent of the jail children's mothers admitted they did not usually see their children's report cards, but no probation mothers admitted a similar failure (table 7-1d). It is certainly possible that more mothers had failed to see report cards than would admit this. Their children, however, were even less apt to disclose that their mother did not see the school reports. The children seemed to realize it was socially disapproved for a parent not to see reports as the school required and they were unwilling to expose the mother's shortcoming in this matter (table 7-1f).

Friends play an important part in a school-aged child's life and so it was not unreasonable to expect a mother would have some knowledge of her child's companions. There was a significant difference in the mothers' ability to name their children's friends (table 7-1e). For example, 10 percent of the jail and 31 percent of the probation children's mothers could accurately give the names of their child's friends. But 81 percent of the jail children's mothers and 60 percent in the probation group gave a single unconfirmed name or no name at all. Again children were less willing than their mothers to admit the mother's lack of knowledge, since 92 percent of the jail and 83 percent of the probation children reported their mothers knew their friends' names (table 7-1g).

In summary, the findings support the hypothesis that jail mothers were less informed than probation mothers about their children's activities and interests.

Discussion

Some attention should be given to the finding that the children, especially jail children, were less willing than their mothers to admit the mother's lack of knowledge about their activities and friends. This observation suggests interesting speculation which, while inconclusive, may contribute to a fuller understanding of the adaptation of a child to the fact that the mother is in jail.

A child lives in a much smaller world than his mother. From an early age his parents assume a prominent role in his life. It is perhaps easier for a mother to see her child as only one aspect of her world than it is for the child to see her as only one aspect of his. To a child a parent should be a dependable source of attention and affection. In a single-parent family when a child is confronted with evidence of his mother's lack of interest in his activities and his friends, it is understandable that he might wish to minimize this inattention to outsiders as well as to himself. The egocentricity of a young child may also help account for this behavior.

This predicament is, of course, not restricted to the children of incarcerated mothers, and the causes and effects go well beyond the limits of this study. What lends immediacy to the case of the jail child is the abruptness with which the mother's attention is taken away. Several jail children expressed indirectly the thought that their mothers would not have committed offenses if they had known it would mean having to leave their children. This illustrates how a child interprets his mother's behavior through his own perception of the situation.

A young child is understandably reluctant to admit even to himself that his mother's actions are autonomous to his existence. The result of this is that often a child creates a false, inflated image of his mother. This self-generated and idealized image of the mother, that is, a mother who gives affection and attention unstintingly, becomes especially important to a jail child while his mother is incarcerated. Most children create at times a similar benevolent mother image, but ordinarily the mother's real presence is there to keep a child's fantasies in check.

This created mother's image is not in and of itself unusual or unhealthy. All children to some extent fantasize about their mother's role. Most mothers, even under the best of circumstances, sometimes find themselves temporarily displaced by or criticized for their failure to live up to their child's idealization of them. In the case of the jail child, this problem can become acute. In the absence of the mother, a child is left to his imagination and may compensate for her absence with an unrealistic mother-image which replaces her. This substitution can lead to emotional and behavioral clashes when the mother returns.

In evaluating the jail mothers' lack of information about their children's activities and friends, it should be remembered that this deficiency does not prove a lack of concern on the part of the mothers. Undoubtedly there are others who would have comparable difficulty with the questions asked. Also there is no way of knowing how these same jail mothers might have answered these questions before their period of incarceration.

What can be said with a great deal of certainty is that most of the jail mothers interviewed did poorly themselves in school and despite profuse expressions of wanting their children to do well in school, the interviews reveal that they did little to further this goal. In fact, the interviews suggest these mothers were more interested in having their children finish school than in having them do well academically. On a day-to-day basis this meant they were concerned that their child remain in school all day and stay out of trouble, rather than with the child's performance as a student. This reveals a pragmatic attitude toward education; that is, it provides supervision for the child during the day and opens job opportunities upon graduation. This concern with ends rather than means may partly explain their limited interest in details of the child's school situation.

8 Child's Knowledge of Mother's Legal Situation

Analysis

The separation of the mother from the child creates some unique problems. When the mother is arrested, she potentially experiences a sequence of events: detention, arraignment, plea negotiations, possibly a trial leading to conviction, sentencing, and serving time. The child is not directly involved in this sequence, but becomes an affected party of the outcome. If the mother is detained after arrest or later sentenced to jail, the resultant separation of mother and child is of considerable consequence to the child. The child is affected, albeit indirectly, by the mother's legal entanglements even if those entanglements are not openly disclosed to the child.

How a child views the legal process in which his mother is involved and what he comprehends about the situation is of importance to the mother-child relationship. Some children were close to the mother's situation and had a good understanding of what was happening. Others had a more limited view so that the mother's situation had an aura of confusion and seemed beyond anyone's control. A few of the children were not even aware of the mother's criminal status. Only by understanding how the child perceives his mother's situation can the effects of her arrest, conviction, and sentence be evaluated.

It was hypothesized that more jail than probation children would have knowledge of their mother's arrest, conviction, and sentence. To explore a child's perceptions, a series of questions was asked about the mother's situation. This area of the interview was approached cautiously. After extensive pretesting a sequence of interview questions was developed to explore a child's knowledge, without revealing any information unknown to the child. The questions were designed to open up discussion of the mother's absence and legal status at various points during the interview. The caution was well justified when some of the mothers, especially in the probation group, insisted upon nondisclosure of their criminal involvement as a condition for allowing their children to participate in the study. The interviewers did not disclose any information unknown to the children, nor pressure them to talk about any topics they were unwilling to discuss. Consequently, the data reflect only information that was willingly discussed by the participants, and therefore could be an underestimation of their actual knowledge.

Significantly more jail than probation children realized their mother was serving a sentence. At the time of the first interviews 82 percent of the jail children compared to only 42 percent of the probation children realized their mother was serving a sentence. Those who appeared uncertain, according to the interviewer's estimate, are excluded from those percentages. Only 5 percent of the jail children appeared to have no knowledge of the mother's legal situation compared to 52 percent of the probation children (table 8-1a).

There are a number of explanations as to why children did not know about their mother's legal status. In some cases the mothers effectively concealed the facts from the children. The most common stories jail mothers told children were that they were going to the hospital or to work. Less frequently stories involved mothers going on vacation, going to school, or staying with relatives. Mothers indicated they concealed the fact they were going to jail or on probation because they felt the children were too young to understand, they were embarrassed but would tell the children later, the deception was the first thing that came to mind, or they feared the children might hate them if they knew of their mother's criminal involvement.

Another reason why some children did not know about their mother's sentence was that, although the mother had told the children about her situation, some of the youngest did not grasp the meaning of her explanation. Furthermore, some children did not acknowledge their awareness of the mother's situation during the interviews. Children who were extremely uncomfortable with a topic were not forced to discuss it. Most of the children, however, did know about their mother's criminal status and the discussion that follows is limited to these children. As a result, the group of probation children is reduced to less than half of the original sample.

Children most frequently learned about their mother's legal dilemma by being present at the arrest: 45 percent of the jail and 40 percent of the probation children had been present at the time (table 8-1b). The arrest was a dramatic event for most of the children and some retold the events with obvious relish. The arrests, as recounted by the children, ranged from police arriving at the door with arrest warrants to late-night drug raids. The descriptions ranged from flat to vividly detailed recollections. Some children watched the arrest placidly, while others became more actively involved, sometimes being questioned and searched. One young child even accompanied the mother to the jail because no other care arrangement was available at the time.

For example, Janine M., 14 years old, was present when her mo r and others were arrested for the sale of heroin in her home. After midnight the police burst into their apartment with guns drawn and put everyone, includ-

Table 8-1
Children's Knowledge of Mothers' Legal Situation

	Jail Children (39)	Probation Children (35)	Significance
a. Child knows mother is in jail or on probation			
Yes	82%(32)	42%(13)	$p<.001$
No	5 (2)	52 (16)	
Uncertain	13 (5)	6 (2)	
b. How child learned of mother's arrest[1]			
Child present at arrest	45%(14)	40% (6)	N.S.
Mother told child	42 (13)	40 (6)	
Someone else told child	10 (3)	20 (3)	
Found out another way	3 (1)	—	
c. Child's recollection of arrest[1]			
Forceful (guns, handcuffs, etc)	24% (7)	36% (4)	N.S.
Nonforceful	45 (13)	27 (3)	
Not described or remembered	31 (9)	36 (4)	
d. Child's understanding of why mother was arrested[1]			
Knows offense charged	70%(23)	80%(12)	N.S.
Knows broke law, but unclear about offense	12 (4)	13 (2)	
Does not understand	18 (6)	7 (1)	
e. Child's response about mother's situation[1]			
Truth, jail or probation	3% (1)	—	$p<.001$
Another story	60 (20)	—	
"I don't know"	15 (5)	7% (1)	
Nothing	12 (4)	20 (3)	
Not asked	9 (3)	73 (11)	

Chi-square (χ^2) tests of statistical significance are used in all tables. N.S. indicates that χ^2 was not significant at the .05 level.

[1]Children not aware of mother's arrest or conviction are omitted. Missing responses are omitted.

ing Janine, against the wall to search them for weapons before searching the house for drugs. Janine's mother was handcuffed and taken with the others down to the police station. Janine was left at home to care for her two younger siblings, aged 6 and 9.

Some of the children became very animated when describing their mother's arrest; others were tearful. For example, 24 percent of the jail and 36 percent of the probation children described their mother's arrest, often in great detail, as involving guns and handcuffs. Such arrests were classified as a show of force on the part of the police. In some cases, the interviewers had the impression the child had told the story before and that it would remain a vivid experience. But 45 percent of the jail and 27 percent of the probation children reported nonforceful or peaceful arrests of their mothers. The remainder of the children did not describe or did not remember the events of the arrest (table 8-1c).

The children's second most frequent source of information about the arrest was the mother herself. Mothers conveyed this information to 42 percent of the jail and 40 percent of the probation children (table 8-1b). These figures include many mothers who initially told a false story, but later told the truth either because the child started asking questions or the mother changed her mind about the utility of keeping it a secret. Some mothers made a point of sitting down with the child and calmly explaining the situation. Others preferred to discuss the matter with adults, in the presence of the child, so the child could pick up the information without having to be told directly. Most of the mothers felt it was unrealistic to think the child would not find out eventually and so concluded it was better they heard the truth at home, directly or indirectly.

A few children found out about the arrest from neighbors or other children. In one instance, a child heard gossip about her mother that was confirmed in a newspaper report. One mother, who did not have a prior record and wanted to avoid discussing the matter with her 7-year-old daughter, arranged to turn herself in on a weekday while the child was in school. When the child returned home in the afternoon, the grandmother was there to pick her up and explain the situation. One woman related that she had asked her parish priest to talk to her daughters after she went to jail.

It is not surprising that more jail than probation children knew about their mother's situation. The fact of the jail mother's absence prompted questions from the children and required some explanation. Since many jail mothers had prior incarcerations, another arrest and conviction were not novel events for the children. It was easier for the probation mothers to avoid the issue of their sentence and to keep their criminal status a secret from their children.

Among children who were aware of the mother's sentence, the extent of their knowledge about the mother's criminal involvement did not differ significantly between the two groups (table 8-1d). Most of the children in both groups were aware of the nature of the charges against the mothers. A slightly higher percentage of the probation children, who were an older subsample of the entire probation group, had a precise understanding of the charges and conviction. In one interesting variation a mother arrested for prostitution, along with her husband who was arrested as her pimp, concealed the actual charges from her children. She explained that she felt her two daughters, aged 9 and 11, were too young to be told the truth, so instead she told them they had been arrested for shoplifting. In most cases, however, the mothers gave reasonably accurate, though often simplified, versions of the charges to the children.

While most of the children understood the nature of their mother's offense, the majority felt the punishment she received was too harsh. Children of both groups who knew about the conviction generally expressed the opinion that the sentence was unfair, though a few of the jail children felt the sentence was justified. One 15-year-old girl reported she felt the mother's six-month jail sentence was "for her own good and should teach her a lesson." This was a girl who related bitterness over her mother having previously sent her to a juvenile facility for "running around" and "incorrigibility."

Although the jail children displayed a high level of awareness of their mother's situation, the children were noticeably unwilling to acknowledge it to their acquaintances. Of the jail children who knew their mother was in jail, over three-fourths reported they would not tell their acquaintances about this. Most of the children dealt with questions concerning their mother's absence with evasions and lies. Over half of these children said they made up another story to tell their friends, such as that their mother was visiting relatives or on vacation. The stories were occasionally creative and at times inconsistent. Others evaded the issue completely. A few jail and the majority of the probation children said they were never asked about their mother (table 8-1*e*).

The hypothesis that more jail than probation children would have knowledge of their mother's arrest, conviction, and sentence has been supported. Since more jail children were aware of the mother's criminal status, it suggests there was greater potential for them to be affected by the information. That is, the mother's criminal record was a factor for most of the jail children, whereas more than half of the probation children were not even aware of their mother's conviction. For children who learned about their mother's criminality, an extra dimension was added to their mother's identity—that of being a person who had broken the law.

Discussion

An examination of jail children's knowledge about their mother's arrest suggests two important areas of consideration: what should a mother tell her children, and what should a child tell others about his mother.

Many of the mothers expressed uncertainty about dealing with the problem of what and how to tell their children about their incarceration. Some subsequent concerns appeared to grow out of their initial handling of this issue. These women would probably be amenable to counseling, and in many cases they openly solicited advice and sought approval for their actions from the interviewer.

On the basis of the interviews it appears that many of the mothers' initial treatment of this issue was unrealistic. They supposed their children could be sheltered from the truth, but in fact eventually practically all the jail children learned of their mother's actual situation. Therefore mothers should be advised to deal with the initial informing of their children in a more open and realistic manner.

Sometimes a mother needlessly created unforeseen problems and anxiety by her attempts at deception. For example, one mother told her 6-year-old son she was going to the hospital for a while. When her child learned that other children could visit their mothers in the hospital, he began to suspect that his mother was dead. His grandmother was unable to convince him otherwise until she told him the truth. This created a problem when the mother was released from jail. She quarreled with her mother and tried to reestablish her story that she really had been hospitalized. The result was the child was confused and unable to clearly verbalize what had happened to his mother. He also expressed some hesitancy in going to his mother for advice and said he would seek out the grandmother instead. It would be misleading to attribute the child's trusting relationship with his grandmother solely to this incident, but apparently it had a contributing effect.

Some mothers who openly acknowledged their situation reported surprise at the complacency with which their children accepted the explanation. Children quite often are willing to ally themselves with their parents when allowed the opportunity to do so. A frank admission by the mother in some cases eliminated further discussion and speculation about her crime by the child. In a few families, children reported being upset by their mother repeatedly mentioning her offenses in the child's presence. One 11-year-old girl said she "did not like to think about her mother like that." Perhaps the mother's candor clashed with the child's idealized image of her. Mothers should be encouraged to evaluate a child's receptiveness, considering the child's age and temperament, before deciding what explanation to give.

Children were generally reluctant to discuss their mother's whereabouts and offense with people outside the family. In most cases the interviewers reported children showed initial hesitation in revealing their mother's whereabouts. Often they would look questioningly at the interviewer before answering. Sometimes it was necessary for the interviewer to tell the child she had seen the mother recently, before the child appeared confortable discussing the mother. This reluctance was reportedly characteristic of how these children dealt with the subject with outsiders. The majority did not tell others about their mothers; those who did tended to distort their discussion with some evasion.

It would perhaps be a mistake to encourage children to discuss their mother's problems with outsiders. Some children considered it a private family matter. Others suggested a certain loyalty was expected by their mother. Nondisclosure may contribute to a sense of family unity but it could also isolate a child from his peers.

The few children who openly acknowledged their mother's crime and conviction outside the family reported being teased and bullied when information about their mother's imprisonment became known. One separated father expressed anxiety at the thought that children at school would taunt his 9-year-old son if it became known that the mother had been arrested for prostitution.

It may not be possible to spare the child completely because of the spread of information throughout a neighborhood. A mother would be well advised to anticipate her child finding out about her conviction and explain the situation in a way appropriate to the child's understanding. If the mother would discuss how she felt about the child talking about her with others, it would help the child resolve the issue for himself and respond to inquiries with some confidence.

9

Visits and Other Contact between Mother and Child

Analysis

Separation from family and children has been reported to be one of the most difficult aspects of incarceration for women (Ward & Kassebaum, 1965; Burkhart, 1973). Visitation is one means by which inmates can try to maintain some relationship with their children. The presence and maintenance of strong family ties is seen by many to be a critical factor in an inmate's successful adjustment after release (Markley, 1973). Visitation may play an important role in helping to maintain these bonds.

Visitation provides some contact in the broken relationships of jailed mothers and children. Frequency of visits and quality of contact are assumed to be important factors. Frequency of visits could be estimated from mothers' reports, and their evaluation of the varied visiting conditions and specific evaluations of their visits were an indication of the quality of visits. Without making any assumptions about the desirabilty of visits for children, the present study tested the hypothesis that the frequency of children's visits would be affected by the child's age, the type of crime the mother was convicted of, the length of her sentence, and the visitation facilities available in county jails.

Frequency of visits was determined to be nonexistent, infrequent, or frequent on the basis of the mother's report of visits with her child. A general notion of what constituted infrequent versus frequent visits had to be adopted because the visiting policies of the jails differed. Since the length of the mothers' sentences varied, the total number of visits likewise varied. Children who visited as often as visitation was available or on a regular basis at least once every week or two were considered frequent visitors. Fewer visits or those on an irregular basis were considered infrequent. The frequency of visits that had occurred to date was determined at the first interview and an overall estimate was made at the second interview, after release (time II).

Age of Child

Children were classified in three groups on the basis of age: 4-8 years old—youngest, 9-13—middle, and 14-18—oldest. The frequency of children's

visits did not vary according to the child's age. At the time of the first interview 47 percent of the children had not visited their mothers, 31 percent
were infrequent visitors, and 22 percent frequent visitors (table 9-1*a*). According to the reduced group of mothers who were interviewed again after
the release (time II), 34 percent of their children had never visited during the
mother's incarceration, 48 percent visited infrequently, and 18 percent
visited frequently (table 9-2*a* through *f*). In summary, approximately two-
thirds of the children visited their mothers at least once while she served her
sentence, but the frequency of a child's visits was not related to the child's
age (table 9-2*a*).

The mothers' feelings about having their children visit did not vary
significantly according to the age of the child. But 38 percent of the mothers
expressed positive feelings, 36 percent negative feelings, and the remainder
ambivalent feelings about children visiting in jail (table 9-1*b*). There were
more positive feelings about having younger children visit and more
negative feelings about older children (table 9-3*a*). Mothers did not differ
significantly in their feelings about having children visit; nor when asked to
recall the most recent visit with their child, was there a significant difference
in their evaluations according to the age of the children (table 9-4*a*).

This study did not include children under age 4, so no comment can be
made about visits with children of less than school age. Visits appear to
have been important in reassuring school-age children about their mother's
welfare. Jail children expressed a number of concerns about their incarcerated mother. Most frequently they mentioned her safety and their
desire for her to get out. For many of the young children, a visit to the jail
was enough to reassure them that the mother was still alive and healthy.
However, the frequency of visits tapered off near the end of the mother's
jail term.

In summary, the age of the children was not significantly related to the
frequency of visits, nor did it influence the mothers' feelings about having
the child visit or their evaluation of the latest visit.

Type of Crime

The women were divided into groups based on the type of crime for which
they had been convicted. The categories were property offenses: lar-
ceny/theft, fraud, forgery, and embezzlement; violent offenses:
manslaughter, assault, and robbery; narcotics offenses: heroin sales,
possession, and drug law violation; and other offenses: prostitution and
perjury.

Some women had been convicted of more than one offense. For the
purpose of these offense groups, they were classified on the basis of the conviction for which they received the longest sentence. Of the jail mothers in

Table 9-1
Summary Information about Visits and Other Contact during Incarceration, from Mothers in Jail at Time I

	Jail Mothers (54)	Jail Mothers by Child (118)
a. Did mother see child during her incarceration?		
No	45%(24)	47%(55)
Yes, infrequently	36 (19)	31 (36)
Yes, regularly	19 (10)	22 (25)
b. Mother's feelings about child's visit in jail		
Negative	33%(17)	36%(40)
Ambivalent	26 (13)	26 (28)
Positive	40 (21)	38 (42)
c. Did mother and child speak on phone?		
No	26%(14)	23%(26)
Yes, infrequently	21 (11)	16 (18)
Yes, frequently	53 (28)	62 (71)
d. Did mother write letters to child?		
No	36%(19)	37%(43)
Yes, infrequently	28 (15)	22 (25)
Yes, frequently	36 (19)	41 (47)
e. Did mother receive letters from child?		
No	62%(33)	62%(71)
Yes, infrequently	19 (10)	17 (20)
Yes, frequently	19 (10)	21 (24)

this analysis, 42 percent were property offenders, 38 percent narcotics offenders, 18 percent violent offenders, and 2 percent convicted of other offenses.

There was a statistically significant difference in the frequency of children's visits for the different offense groups. Violent offenders had the most frequent visits, with 56 percent of the children visiting frequently. In contrast, only 10 percent of the children of property offenders visited frequently and 52 percent did not visit their mother at all during her incarceration (table 9-2b).

One possible explanation why property offenders received so few visits can be found in their own attitudes about their crimes. For example, Dorothy R. had done housekeeping work in a hospital to help support her unemployed husband and three children, a daughter aged 18 and two sons,

Table 9-2
Visitation by Jail Children

| | Frequency of Visits | | | |
	None (17)	Infrequent (24)	Frequent (9)	Significance
a. Age of child				
4-8	30% (7)	48%(11)	22% (5)	N.S.
9-13	25 (4)	56 (9)	19 (3)	
14-18	55 (6)	36 (4)	9 (1)	
b. Mother's offense				
Property	52%(11)	38% (8)	10% (2)	$p<.005$
Violent	33 (3)	11 (1)	56 (5)	
Narcotics	10 (2)	79 (15)	10 (2)	
Other	100 (1)	—	—	
c. Length of mother's sentence				
30 days or less	—	100% (1)	—	$p<.001$
30-90 days	63%(15)	29 (7)	8% (2)	
90 days-6 mos.	10 (1)	90 (9)	—	
6 mos.-1 year	10 (1)	60 (6)	30 (3)	
More than 1 year	—	20 (1)	80 (4)	
d. County				
Alameda	18% (3)	47% (8)	35% (6)	$p<.02$
San Francisco	55 (11)	45 (9)	—	
San Mateo	50 (3)	33 (2)	17 (1)	
Santa Clara	—	71 (5)	29 (2)	
e. Phone calls between mother and child				
None	73% (8)	18% (2)	9% (1)	$p<.04$
Infrequent	12 (1)	62 (5)	25 (2)	
Frequent	26 (8)	55 (17)	19 (6)	
f. Correspondence between mother and child				
None	83%(10)	8% (1)	8% (1)	$p<.005$
Infrequent	20 (3)	53 (8)	27 (4)	
Frequent	17 (4)	65 (15)	17 (4)	

Note: Information from jail mothers interviewed at time I and II, by child.
Chi-square (χ^2) tests of statistical significance are used in all tables. N.S. indicates that χ^2 was not significant at the .05 level.

aged 8 and 15. Dorothy was convicted of welfare fraud for claiming and collecting welfare payments for an extra, nonexistent child. She had no prior adult criminal record and her family had been unaware of her illicit claim. She was sentenced to six months in jail and ordered to make restitution. When her father visited her during the first week of the sentence, she reported being very embarrassed and asked her father not to allow her children to see her behind bars. Her father, who was caring for the children, complied with her request and agreed it would probably be damaging to the

Table 9-3

Mothers' Feelings about Having Child Visit, Time I (Jail Mothers by Child—118)

	Negative	Mixed	Positive	Significance
a. Child's age				
4-8	33%(17)	24%(12)	43%(22)	N.S.
9-13	33 (12)	28 (10)	39 (14)	
14-18	55 (11)	30 (6)	15 (3)	
b. Mother's offense				
Property	45%(28)	23%(14)	32%(20)	N.S.
Violent	6 (1)	33 (6)	61 (11)	
Narcotics	36 (10)	29 (8)	36 (10)	
Other	33 (1)	33 (1)	33 (1)	
c. Mother's sentence				
30 days or less	17% (2)	8% (1)	75% (9)	$p < .001$
30-90 days	43 (14)	25 (8)	31 (10)	
90 days-6 mos.	64 (23)	17 (6)	19 (7)	
6 mos.-1 year	—	19 (3)	81 (13)	
More than 1 year	—	77 (10)	23 (3)	
d. Time served				
30 days or less	39%(10)	19% (5)	42%(11)	$p < .001$
30-90 days	38 (15)	32 (13)	30 (12)	
90 days to 6 mos.	60 (15)	—	40 (10)	
6 mos. to 1 year	—	36 (5)	64 (9)	
More than 1 year	—	100 (5)	—	
e. County				
Alameda	23% (6)	38%(10)	38%(10)	$p < .001$
San Francisco	72 (20)	14 (4)	14 (4)	
San Mateo	44 (7)	44 (7)	12 (2)	
Santa Clara	18 (7)	18 (7)	65 (26)	
f. Mother saw child during her incarceration				
No	59%(29)	4% (2)	37%(18)	$p < .001$
Yes, frequently	31 (11)	22 (8)	47 (17)	
Yes, regularly	—	72 (18)	28 (7)	
g. Mother's evaluation of visits				
Negative	50% (6)	50% (6)	—	$p < .001$
Mixed	10 (2)	40 (8)	50%(10)	
Positive	10 (3)	38 (11)	52 (15)	
Does not apply, no visits	62 (29)	2 (1)	36 (17)	

Chi-square (χ^2) tests of statistical significance are used in all tables. N.S. indicates that χ^2 was not significant at the .05 level.

children to see her in jail. Dorothy's greatest fear was that her children would hate her when she got out. In fact, after her release, the two older children reported that they no longer trusted their mother.

Most mothers convicted of narcotics offenses had visits with their

Table 9-4

Mothers' Evaluation of Recent Visit with Child in Jail, Time I (Jail Mothers by Child—118)

	Negative	Mixed	Positive	Does Not Apply	Significance
a. Child's age					
4-8	8% (4)	21%(11)	27%(14)	44%(23)	N.S.
9-13	8 (3)	15 (6)	32 (13)	45 (18)	
14-18	23 (5)	14 (3)	9 (2)	54 (12)	
b. Mother's offense					
Property	—	23%(14)	24%(15)	53%(33)	p .001
Violent	22% (5)	22 (5)	—	56 (13)	
Narcotics	27 (7)	4 (1)	54 (14)	15 (4)	
Other	—	—	—	100 (3)	
c. Length of sentence					
Less than 30 days	—	8% (1)	17% (2)	75%(24)	p .001
30-90	3% (1)	18 (6)	18 (6)	61 (20)	
90 days-6 mos.	21 (6)	18 (5)	29 (8)	32 (9)	
6 mos.-1 year	—	50 (8)	50 (8)	—	
More than 1 year	50 (5)	—	50 (5)	—	
d. County					
Alameda	19% (5)	23% (6)	27% (7)	31% (8)	p .005
San Francisco	18 (6)	6 (2)	6 (2)	69 (22)	
San Mateo	6 (1)	31 (5)	18 (3)	44 (7)	
Santa Clara	—	18 (7)	43 (17)	40 (16)	

Chi-square (χ^2) tests of statistical significance are used in all tables. N.S. indicates that χ^2 was not significant at the .05 level.

children. The mothers' drug involvement, typically both sales and use, was generally known to their children. Cathy L., a young mother with two children, had been dealing heroin out of her house for over a year. Occasionally the children acted as lookouts for patrol cars and strangers when she was making a sale. She insisted she never introduced anyone to heroin but only supplied it to friends who needed it. Cathy and her children appeared to accept her arrest as a hazard of her involvement in drug traffic. She was self-righteous about her role selling narcotics and justified it as a means of supporting her children.

Yvonne B. is an example of a violent offender who was convicted of manslaughter. She shot her common-law husband, who was also the father of three of her six children, including a daughter born while she was in jail. The children were present at the time of the shooting, which occurred in the house, and remained when the police and ambulance arrived. The man died the following morning in the hospital. All the children visited her in jail. Yvonne reports these visits were very upsetting to the children and herself and consequently she allowed them to come only every two weeks. She wanted the children to visit but disliked upsetting them and herself. No physical contact is allowed at Santa Rita and Yvonne was particularly disturbed about her inability to hold her infant. The children generally reported that it was good to see their mother but that it made them unhappy.

Caution should be used when interpreting these cases. Generalizations should be avoided because each case has distinguishing elements.

Length of Sentence

Sentences served in county jails were categorized by length into units of thirty to ninety days, ninety days to six months, six months to one year, and more than one year. The most common length of sentence was thirty to ninety days, which accounted for 48 percent of the jail mothers. The categories of offenses were broad and include a range of crimes. There was not a significant relationship between category of offense and length of sentence (table 9-5).

There was a significant difference in frequency of children's visits according to the length of the mother's sentence. Mothers with relatively long sentences of more than half a year had the most frequent visits and those with sentences of less than ninety days had infrequent or no visits (table 9-2c). Mothers with short sentences often felt it was better for the children not to visit them in jail. The mothers also assumed they could get along without having to see the children for a short period of separation. Most acknowledged they would want to see their children if they had to serve any more time. A few mothers with longer sentences had planned not to have the children visit, but changed their minds after spending some time in jail. Some mothers yielded to the child's request and others satisfied their own growing desire to see the children.

County Jail Facilities

All the jails were county facilities used typically for misdemeanants with sentences of less than one year. The county in which a woman was arrested was also where she served her sentence. For purposes of description and discussion, it is useful to consider the four county jails individually. (Additional information describing the jails is included in Appendix I.)

Santa Clara County (Elmwood). This is a single-story structure which did not have the exterior appearance of a jail, and visitors did not see cells. There was a variety of jail clothing available. It was located ten miles from the metropolitan area and public transportation was within one half mile.

Visiting consisted of two forms: contact visiting available Sunday morning, and visitation behind glass with phones available on some weekdays. For frequency of visits, all the mothers had visits with children (table 9-2d).

Table 9-5
Jail Mothers' Sentences by Offense Category

	Property	Violent	Narcotics	Other	Significance
Jail sentence					
30 days or less	71%(5)	14%(1)	—	14%(1)	N.S.
30-90 days	43 (9)	19 (4)	33%(7)	5 (1)	
90 days-6 mos.	69 (9)	—	23 (3)	8 (1)	
6 mos.-1 year	44 (4)	11 (1)	44 (4)	—	
Over 1 year	33 (1)	33 (1)	33 (1)	—	

Chi-square (χ^2) tests of statistical significance are used in all tables. N.S. indicates that χ^2 was not significant at the .05 level.

Mothers generally gave positive evaluations of their recent visits and the visiting conditions (tables 9-3*e* and 9-4*d*). This was the only facility in the study with contact visiting; that is, the inmate and visitor could physically touch each other. Some mothers only allowed their children to visit during the contact visitation period on Sundays because they wanted to avoid exposing them to the visitation conditions with bulletproof glass and telephones which existed throughout the rest of the week. There were complaints about the contact visiting being on Sunday mornings because families which attended church services were thus denied these visits.

Alameda County (Santa Rita). This facility is located out of town in a large correctional complex, with a guard station at the entry and signs and warnings posted. It is thirty miles from the metropolitan area; there is no public transportation.

Visitation consisted of separation of visitors from inmates by long tables, with no contact allowed across the table. For frequency of visits, approximately half of the children made infrequent visits; 18 percent of the mothers had no visits, and 35 percent had frequent visits (table 9-2*d*).

The mothers' attitudes about having children visit were 38 percent positive, 38 percent mixed, and 23 percent negative (table 9-3*e*). The substantial distance visitors were required to travel did not appear to present a major problem. Most of the mothers' complaints were that they wished they could touch the children (table 9-4*d*).

San Mateo County. This is a maximum security jail located in a high-rise government building, and the only urban jail in the study.

Visitation consisted of isolation behind bulletproof glass and having phones (with recording devices); the visiting schedule was reduced during the study. For frequency of visits, half of the mothers' children did not visit and one-third were infrequent visitors (table 9-2*d*).

Only 12 percent of the mothers had positive feeings about having their children visit them in jail, 44 percent had negative feelings, and 44 percent had mixed feelings (table 9-3e). Mothers who expressed acceptance of the high-security visitation facilities mentioned their fear that contact visits would create a much greater threat of contraband, such as weapons and drugs, being smuggled into the jail by other inmates. There was uneasiness among the women in this facility, which they blamed in part on the crowded quarters with eight women per cell and temporarily because of the increased security due to the presence of a notorious federal prisoner (Patricia Hearst).

San Francisco County (San Bruno). This facility is located outside the county in San Bruno. Isolated and old, it stands next to a fortresslike men's jail. Guards are stationed at the entry.

Visitation consisted of separation by two thick screens, with a small glass panel to see through. Because of the height of the glass panel, the arrangement is awkward for children. There is no privacy and conversations sometimes had to be shouted to be heard over the sound of others. For frequency of visits, mothers had the lowest overall rate of visiting, 55 percent had no visits at all and none had frequent visits (table 9-2d).

The mothers' reactions to having children visit under the current visiting conditions were overwhelmingly negative (table 9-3e). Only 6 percent evaluated their most recent visit as a positive experience for both the mother and child (table 9-4d). Mothers in this jail typically did not encourage their children to visit. Transportation to the jail presented a problem for some because no public transportation was available from San Francisco.

Several mothers had had previous experience in one or more of these jails or with correctional institutions outside the scope of the study. One woman when recounting her prior incarcerations remarked that the quality of life in Elmwood had improved in terms of better food and clothing during the detention of a well-known federal prisoner (Angela Davis) a few years earlier. Elmwood, the Santa Clara County facility, always fared well in comparison with the other Bay Area jails. In contrast, San Francisco's jail was invariably considered the least desirable local jail in which to serve time. One mother had served time in a southern jail, and another had been in several facilities in New York; both described the local jail conditions as better, with special reference to their cleanliness. However, the jails in this study suffered in comparison to the California prisons in which a few women had served time or had heard about from friends. As is generally true of county jails, they were described as more crowded and as having fewer programs and activities than state or federal prisons.

Other Forms of Contact

In addition to visitation, other forms of contact between mother and child were by telephone and mail (table 9-1c, *d,* and *e*). Telephone contact could only be instigated by the mother because incoming calls to inmates were not permitted in any of the jails. Accessibility of phones varied among the jails and sometimes from week to week within a jail. In one jail a phone was generally available, subject only to the use of other inmates and time limits imposed on conversations. In San Mateo there was a single pay phone with only one reusable dime available for its use. If, as happened once during the study, the dime was lost or taken, no one could use the phone until the return or replacement of the dime. When the phone was available, the women were limited to one ten-minute call per day. The least desirable situation existed in San Francisco, where inmates could phone only under the supervision of a staff person in the jail office. Chronic understaffing usually limited the women to one call a week. General uncertainties in placing the call and reaching the person reduced the actual number of successful phone calls. The most difficult circumstances were posed by the children who lived in homes that did not have telephone service. It was interesting to observe that when jail children were asked if their mother knew what they were doing, they usually reported her knowledge of their activities on the basis of phone contact the mother had with family members.

Writing letters was a relatively uncommon form of communication between mothers and children. More than one-third of the mothers never wrote to their children and approximately 62 percent never received letters from their children (tables 9-1d and e). If there were no letters or phone calls between a mother and a child, it was unlikely there would be any visits (table 9-2e and f).

The hypothesis about the frequency of children's visits was supported in three parts, but not in the fourth. Although the age of the child was not related to the frequency of the child's visits, such factors as type of crime, length of sentence, and the county facility were all significantly related to the frequency of visits. Children of all ages were just as likely to visit their mothers, but were more apt to visit if the mother were a narcotics or violent offender rather than a property offender. The probability of visits was higher if the mother was serving a longer sentence than one for less than ninety days. There were substantial differences in the jail facilities and policies in the four counties, and there was a significant difference in the frequency of visits by children depending on where the mother was serving her sentence.

Discussion

The question of visitation presents several complicated issues that require consideration. What effect does visiting a mother in jail have on a child? Who should determine whether a child visits? Should children be encouraged to visit their mothers in jail?

Advantages & disadvantages.

Most jail visitation facilities were physically oppressive. They were designed for secure adult visitation, without specific consideration for children. In fact, until recently some institutions did not allow visits by children under age 18. Children were treated the same as adult visitors in the four jails in this study.

Mothers reported that children were most satisfied with visits when physical contact was allowed and visits were longer than ten minutes. When there was no contact and visits were brief, children exhibited their distress by crying and resisting leaving. It would seem a simple matter for jail authorities to consider the predicament of young children as visitors. The facilities could be made less restrictive for children and visits could be lengthened.

A mother's attitude toward visitation is extremely important in establishing a favorable atmosphere. A mother who seeks to reassure her child of her well-being and her continued concern for the child will quite likely promote a beneficial effect for the child. A visit with a mother who expresses self-interest and self-pity could be unnecessarily stressful for a young child. Mothers tend to have mixed motives for wanting visits, and it is difficult to predict the impact of any given visit on an individual child.

Mothers who were generally cheerful and enthusiastic tended to report satisfactory visits, while mothers who were upset and had emotional outbursts created upsetting visits for the children. Visits were often temporarily disturbing for children, regardless of the mother's demeanor, especially when they had to leave.

Some women felt it would be selfish to have their children visit. They wanted to see their children, but thought it might be harmful to them. In one case a woman's boyfriend brought her child to visit as a surprise against her wishes. She reported the visit was pleasant for both of them, despite her initial reluctance, and she wanted to see the child again. Another mother reported great anger when her separated husband brought their child to see her in jail. The mother felt he had done this to expose her to the child in a humiliating situation because he planned to remarry and to obtain permanent custody of the child. This father apparently used visitation for his own purposes at the expense of the mother, without considering its effect on the child.

No standard practice was evident in determining whether a child was allowed to visit. The mother in jail, the temporary caretaker, and even the child could all have conflicting interests as to whether or not there were visits. If a temporary guardian was trying to win the affection of the child from the mother, visits were not made. In one foster-care situation the guardian did not permit visits because she felt it would be detrimental for a young child.

Further research is necessary to determine the long-term effects, if any, brought about by visiting a parent in jail. One woman adamantly refused to have her child visit, because as a young girl she had visited her father in this very jail and had been quite upset by the experience. Whatever real effects her childhood experience might have had, the intensity of her memory suggests that it was traumatic.

In addition to a child's age and temperament, the length of sentence and the probability of reunion afterward should be considered when making a decision about visits. If a child is not to be reunited with the mother, there seems little point in subjecting him to jail visits. If a mother is serving only a short sentence, visitation is probably not essential. But if a woman has a long jail sentence and plans to be reunited with her child, visits could be of value in reassuring the child and helping them maintain some continuous relationship. With improved jail facilities and policies and a thoughtful attitude on the part of the mother, visitation can be a beneficial experience for the child.

10 Child's Legal Socialization

Analysis

By school age, all children have some awareness of the police and their activities. The police are conspicuous figures of legal authority, and a child's impression of them is likely to influence his orientation toward the legal system. A person's opinions change over time with maturity and experience, but early experience may have an enduring influence on future attitudes. One concern is that children of incarcerated parents may develop a negative orientation to the legal system that continues into adolescence and adulthood and might increase the likelihood of their delinquency.

It was hypothesized that jail children would have more experience with the legal system and more negative attitudes toward the police than probation children. The subject of a child's orientation toward the legal system was examined in three parts: experiences with the legal system, attitudes toward the police, and level of legal reasoning. Given the age range of the children in this study, examination of their attitudes and reasoning was limited to asking hypothetical questions and to comparing their responses with preestablished norms.

Experiences

It was expected that children of convicted parents would have more experience with the legal system than other children. These contacts with the criminal justice system were potentially of a personal nature and potentially negative in outcome. Several possible sources of contact were explored: (1) presence at an arrest, particularly the mother's arrest; (2) attendance at a court session, particularly involving the mother's alleged criminal activity; (3) a visit to a correctional institution, in this case jail children's visits to the county jail where the mother was incarcerated; and (4) personal involvement with the police.

There was a significant difference between the groups of interviewed children in whether or not they had witnessed their own mother's arrest: 38 percent of the jail and 21 percent of the probation children were present. Another smaller group, 15 percent of the jail and 14 percent of the probation children, were not present but had some recollection of the arrest (table 10-1a).

Table 10-1
Children's Experience with Legal System

	Jail Children	Probation Children	Significance
a. Child's recollection of mother's arrest or self-surrender			
Child present	38%(15)	21% (6)	$p<.005$
Child remembers, but not present	15 (6)	14 (4)	
Does not remember	31 (12)	7 (2)	
Child not aware	15 (6)	57 (16)	
b. Child's impression of mother's arrest			
Forceful	18% (7)	14% (4)	$p<.01$
Not forceful	33 (13)	4 (1)	
Not remember or not aware	49 (19)	82 (23)	
c. Child's experience witnessing arrests			
No	9% (3)	31% (9)	$p<.02$
Yes, someone not known	29 (10)	38 (11)	
Yes, someone known, friend	3 (1)	7 (2)	
Yes, family member	60 (21)	24 (7)	
d. Child's experience in court			
Yes	62%(24)	53%(10)	N.S.
No	38 (15)	47 (9)	
e. Child ever in trouble with police			
Yes	24% (9)	17% (5)	N.S.
No	76 (28)	83 (25)	

	Age of Child			Significance
	4-8	9-13	14-18	
f. Jail and probation child's experience witnessing arrests				
No	29% (8)	14% (4)	—	$p<.04$
Yes, someone not known	25 (7)	43 (12)	25% (2)	
Yes, someone known, friend	—	4 (1)	25 (2)	
Yes, family member	46 (13)	39 (11)	50 (4)	
g. Jail children's experience witnessing arrests				
No	20% (3)	—	—	N.S.
Yes, someone not known	27 (4)	31% (4)	29% (2)	
Yes, someone known	—	—	14 (1)	
Yes, family member	53 (8)	69 (9)	57 (4)	

Table 10-1 *(continued)*
Children's Experience with Legal System

	Age of Child			
	4-8	9-13	14-18	Significance
h. Probation children's experience witnessing arrests				
No	38% (5)	27% (4)	—	p < .01
Yes, someone not known	23 (3)	53 (8)	—	
Yes, someone known	—	7 (1)	100% (1)	
Yes, family member	38 (5)	13 (2)	—	
i. Jail and probation child, ever been in trouble with police				
No	86%(25)	77%(23)	62.5% (5)	p < .01
Yes, minor	14 (4)	23 (7)	12.5 (1)	
Yes, juvenile court	—	—	12.5 (1)	
Yes, major	—	—	12.5 (1)	

Chi-square (χ^2) tests of statistical significance are used in all tables. N.S. indicates that χ^2 was not significant at the .05 level.

When the children were asked to give their impressions of the mother's arrest, 18 percent of the jail and 14 percent of the probation children mentioned the use of drawn guns, handcuffs, or rough treatment by the police (table 10-1*b*).

The children were asked whether they had ever seen anyone else arrested. Considerably more children in both groups reported having seen some such arrest: 91 percent of the jail and 69 percent of the probation children. Of those who had witnessed an arrest, 69 percent of the jail and 45 percent of the probation children had seen a person they knew arrested (table 10-1*c*). When asked to describe what they had seen, children often gave dramatic accounts. There was considerable variety in the circumstances and settings of these arrests. Some arrests took place in the children's homes, some were on school premises, but most were in their neighborhoods.

It was assumed that older children were more likely to have seen an arrest than younger children. When the two groups were considered jointly, this proved to be true, with all children over age 13 having witnessed an arrest (table 10-1*f*). When the two groups were analyzed separately, there was a significant difference by age for the probation group but not for the jail group. That is, an older probation child was more likely to have witnessed an arrest than a younger probation child. In contrast, a jail child of any age typically had seen an arrest (table 10-1*g* and *h*).

The children's experiences in court did not differ between the groups (table 10-1*d*). Most of the children had been to a hearing, usually with their mother. Their understanding of what happens in court increased with age. Older children could more accurately explain what judges and lawyers do and the function of the judicial process in general. In an isolated case, three brothers reported having testified in court during a custody hearing that was held after their mother had been accused of child abuse and neglect. The boys' grandmother had reported her daughter-in-law to the police and the mother eventually pled guilty to related criminal charges and to contributing to the delinquency of minors. The three boys' willingness to discuss this experience varied; the middle child, aged 10, readily related the experience and told how he answered all the questions in court, while the older and younger brothers were reluctant to discuss it. The judge removed the boys from the mother's care, placing them in separate foster homes.

In the jail children group 66 percent had visited their mothers at some time during her term in jail. These visits ranged from once to frequent and took place in facilities which ranged from maximum security jails with bulletproof glass enclosures to supervised visits in jails where physical contact was permitted.

When jail children were asked while their mother was in jail, "do you know what it's like inside a jail?" over half gave a negative description and most of the others said they did not know what a jail was like. For further details of jail children's experiences visiting their mothers in jail see chapter 9.

When asked if they personally had ever been in trouble with the police, there was not a significant difference between the two groups. The majority of the children had not (table 10-1e). This was not surprising given the young age of most of the children. A few older children reported having been in some minor trouble with the police (table 10-1i).

The jail group had somewhat greater exposure to the police and legal system than the probation group in that more jail children had witnessed arrests, including their mother's arrest, and visited their mothers in jail. There was, however, no significant difference between the groups in whether they had ever been in court or had been involved with the police due to their own delinquency.

Attitudes   towards police

In an attempt to probe the attitudes of these children concerning their image of the police, they were asked a series of hypothetical questions. These questions dealt with whether they would seek the assistance of an available police officer or report potentially dangerous or criminal activities. The children were asked what they would do in the following situations, assuming a police officer were nearby:

1. If they were lost and needed instructions
2. If they were hurt and needed help
3. If they saw a bank robber fleeing a bank with a bag of money
4. If they saw a man walking down the street with a gun
5. If they saw adults fighting and it looked like someone would get hurt.

There were no significant differences between the two groups of children in what they said their actions would be in these hypothetical situations (table 10-2a through e). In all five situations the majority of the children said they would contact the police officer. However, there were age trends in the children's responses. In the situation where a child was injured, there was an increasing willingness with age to ask an officer for help. In the situations where the child witnessed a crime or potential injury of someone else, there was decreasing willingness to report the incidents to the police by the older children. This reluctance of the older children was expressed in a number of ways.

For example, in response to the question, "what would you do if you

Table 10-2
Children's Attitudes toward the Police

Would Child Seek Assistance of or Report to Police	Jail Children	Probation Children	Significance
a. If lost and needed instructions			
Yes	96%(25)	94%(30)	N.S.
No	4 (1)	6 (2)	
Does not know	—	—	
b. If hurt and needed help			
Yes	88%(22)	87%(27)	N.S.
No	12 (3)	13 (4)	
Does not know	—	—	
c. If saw bankrobber fleeing			
Yes	67%(16)	87%(26)	N.S.
No	25 (6)	13 (4)	
Does not know	8 (2)	—	
d. If saw man with gun			
Yes	67%(18)	88%(28)	N.S.
No	30 (8)	12 (4)	
Does not know	4 (1)	—	
e. If saw adults fighting			
Yes	64%(16)	70%(21)	N.S.
No	32 (8)	27 (8)	
Does not know	4 (1)	3 (1)	

Table 10-2 *(continued)*

| Jail and Probation Children | Age of Child | | | |
Combined by Age	4-8	9-13	14-18	Significance
f. If saw man with gun				
Yes	88%(21)	79%(23)	33% (2)	p<.01
No	12 (3)	21 (6)	50 (3)	
Does not know	—	—	17 (1)	
g. If saw bankrobber fleeing				
Yes	95%(20)	71%(20)	40% (2)	p<.04
No	5 (1)	25 (7)	40 (2)	
Does not know	—	4 (1)	20 (1)	

	Jail Children	Probation Children	Significance
h. Does child want to become police officer			
Yes	28% (9)	38%(12)	N.S.
No	50 (16)	50 (16)	
Does not know	22 (7)	12 (4)	

| | Age of Child | | | |
	4-8	9-13	14-18	Significance
i. Does child want to become police officer? (jail and probation combined by age)				
Yes	41%(12)	28% (8)	17% (1)	N.S.
No	45 (13)	55 (16)	50 (3)	
Does not know	14 (4)	17 (5)	33 (2)	

	Boys	Girls	Significance
j. Does child want to become police officer? (jail and probation combined by sex)			
Yes	41%(13)	25% (8)	N.S.
No	41 (13)	59 (19)	
Does not know	19 (6)	16 (5)	

	Jail Children	Probation Children	Significance
k. Child's feelings about police			
Positive	40%(15)	46%(15)	N.S.
Mixed	27 (10)	33 (11)	
Negative	32 (12)	21 (7)	

Table 10-2 *(continued)*

| | Impression of Police | | | |
	Positive	Mixed	Negative	Significance
l. Jail and probation children combined experience witnessing arrest				
Yes, someone known	29% (6)	33% (7)	38% (8)	N.S.
Yes, someone unknown	46 (11)	25 (6)	29 (7)	
Never	61 (11)	28 (5)	11 (2)	
m. Jail children's presence at mother's arrest				
Child present	33% (5)	20% (3)	47% (7)	N.S.
Not present	41 (7)	35 (6)	24 (4)	
Not aware	60 (3)	20 (1)	20 (1)	

| | Want to Become Police Officer | | | |
	Yes	Unsure	No	Significance
n. Probation children's experience in court				
Yes	71% (5)	14% (1)	14% (1)	$p < .05$
No	17 (2)	17 (2)	67 (8)	
o. Jail children's experience in court				
Yes	7% (2)	38% (9)	54% (13)	N.S.
No	33 (5)	13 (2)	54 (8)	

Chi-square (χ^2) tests of statistical significance are used in all tables. N.S. indicates that χ^2 was not significant at the .05 level.

saw a man walking down the street with a gun?'' some older children suggested that they would simply get out of the way to avoid getting hurt (table 10-2*f*). It should be pointed out that seeing someone carrying a gun was not a novel situation for some of these children to consider, but could have been based on actual experience. The children in one family had recently encountered a similar situation. They responded by repeating their mother's firm instructions that if they heard gunshots, they were to run home or into a neighbor's house. If seeking shelter would expose them to danger, they had been instructed to fall to the ground. Several shootings had recently occurred in their neighborhood. Other children stated that if someone were carrying a gun, it was none of their business and they would not get involved or notify a police officer.

In the situation of the fleeing bank robber there was also a decreased willingness with age to report the crime to the police (table 10-2*g*). This question met with enthusiasm from some of the children who said they would cheer the robber on or help him get away. One boy even suggested that perhaps he could share in the loot since, by his silence, he would be helping the robber escape detection. Others, usually older, said they were not going to help the police do their job.

When children were asked if they would like to be police officers when they grew up, there was not a significant difference between the groups or by age or sex. Half of the children in both the jail and probation groups did not want to become police officers (table 10-2*h*). There was decreasing interest with age (table 10-2*i*), and fewer girls wanted to become police officers (table 10-2*j*).

When children were asked the more abstract question, "how do you feel about the police?" there were again no significant differences between the groups by age or sex. Most of the children gave positive responses to the question (table 10-2*k*).

To explore the idea that children with different backgrounds would have different attitudes toward the legal system, experiential factors were used. Children's attitudes about the police were analyzed according to their personal experiences. Several trends were observed. Considering both groups together, those who had more contact with the police also tended to have more negative attitudes. Children who had witnessed arrests, especially of someone they knew, were least likely to have positive impressions of the police (table 10-2*l*). Jail children who had witnessed their mother's arrest most often had negative impressions, and none of the children who witnessed any rough treatment by the police during the mother's arrest wanted to become police officers themselves (table 10-2*m*).

When the children's experience in court was compared with their desire to become police officers, there was a dramatic difference between the two groups: 71 percent of the probation group but only 7 percent of the jail children wanted to be police officers (table 10-2*n* and *o*).

To investigate whether a relationship existed between a child's overall experience with the police and his attitude toward them, scales were developed to establish summary scores for the children. Individual experiences were weighted according to the immediacy of the situation so that being present at the mother's arrest was more heavily weighted than seeing a stranger arrested. Children's responses to attitude questions were combined with more emphasis given to a child's direct opinion about the police and less for his willingness to report incidents to the police.

There were positive correlations between age and experience for jail as well as probation boys and girls. Jail children aged 10 and older typically had considerable experience with the police. About half of the younger jail and virtually all the probation children had less experience (figure 10-1). There were few teenagers in the probation group so that group was mostly

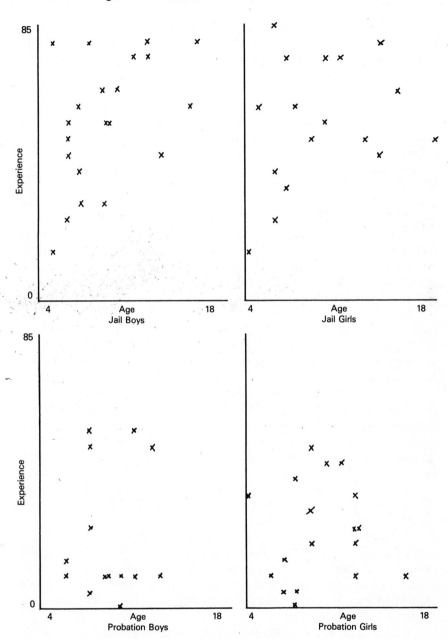

Figure 10-1. Children's Experience by Age

younger children. Jail children of all ages had greater opportunities for exposure to the police and the legal system because it was usually possible for them to visit their mothers in jail and often their mothers had previously been arrested and served time.

Over half of the children in both groups and for both sexes had an overall positive orientation toward the police. There were negative correlations between age and attitude for all except jail girls (figure 10-2). The fact that older jail girls were more positive in their attitudes while other older children were more negative toward the police was noteworthy.

Jail girls under age 10 were split between positive and negative attitudes. With one exception, girls aged 13 and over expressed relatively positive attitudes. The situations of these girls and their reactions to the mother's incarceration are revealing. A girl of 18 who had recently graduated from high school and had planned to attend a trade school was obliged to stay at home and care for her five younger siblings while her mother was incarcerated. Another teenaged girl was unhappy about having less freedom and more responsibility while her mother was in jail. One girl aspired to become a police officer. She was self-righteous and made it clear that her mother had slipped to a low point in her estimation. One girl did not desire to visit her mother because she did "not want to see her in a place like that." A 15-year-old girl expressed some satisfaction that her mother was in jail so that she could see what it was like. This girl had previously been placed in a juvenile institution at her mother's request for being incorrigible.

The mother's incarceration had direct and undesired consequences for these girls. The added responsibilities they had to assume reduced their own free time. Perhaps these obligations also disposed them to have a less tolerant view of the mother and her criminal activities which resulted in her present inability to meet her maternal responsibilities. In conjunction with this resentful attitude about the mother the jail girls had more favorable opinions about the police. None of the jail boys or probation children were required to assume domestic responsibilities as a result of the mother's conviction.

The 14-year-old girl who was the only older jail girl expressing a negative attitude toward the police had been involved in her mother's arrest during a drug raid in their home. A police officer tore a pocket on her blouse, and she viewed herself as a coparticipant with her mother. She felt her mother had been tricked and victimized by the police and expressed resentment toward them.

Overall there was a negative correlation between experience and attitude; that is, with more experience the children tended to have less favorable attitudes toward the police. Analysis was done separately for jail

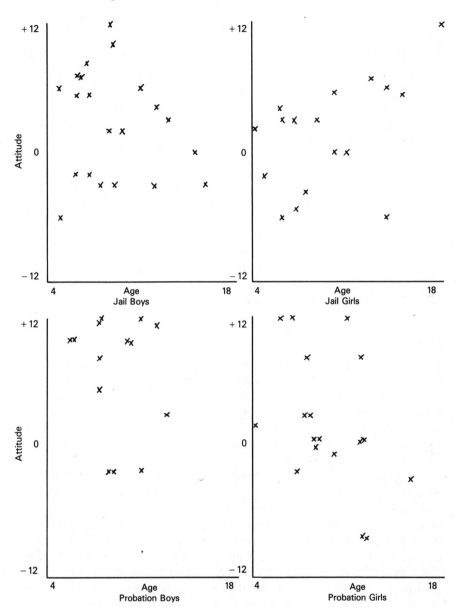

Figure 10-2. Children's Attitude by Age

and probation children and for boys and girls, and only probation boys did not fit this pattern (figure 10-3).

Age, however, was a confounding variable because most older children had more experience as well as more negative attitudes. Multiple regression was used to measure the simultaneous influence of age and experience upon attitude. To examine the relationship of experience to attitude while controlling for the influence of age, the predicted values were subtracted from the observed data and the residuals were plotted. The correlation between residuals for experience and attitude was $r = -.69$ for jail and $r = .11$ for probation children. The graphs show a tendency for jail children's attitudes to be positive when they have relatively little experience with the police and to become negative when they have more experience (figure 10-4). No such relationship exists for the probation children, for whom the range of experience is lower.

Children who had negative experiences with the police were more reluctant to call them for assistance and had less confidence in them. The negative attitudes of the experienced children could also reflect their growing awareness of community sentiments.

Levels of Legal Reasoning

To evaluate the legal reasoning of offenders' children, a series of questions was asked that allowed comparison with other children (table 10-3). It was anticipated that children with more direct experiences with police and the legal system would have different styles of legal reasoning than those of the same ages without such experiences. The Tapp and Levine typology of legal-reasoning levels was used in examining this area (Tapp & Levine, 1970, 1974; Tapp & Kohlberg, 1971).

Tapp and Levine have proposed a sociopsychological developmental model designed to describe and analyze the legal reasoning of individuals. Their empirical research has concentrated on the structure of reasoning processes and the definition of legal issues. They developed a legal-levels typology based on the assumption that stages of individual development are characterized by distinctive ways of thinking about legal values. The typology was derived from an interpretation of responses to open-ended questions about law and justice that were administered to children of various ages. The configuration of legal reasoning that emerged from the analysis of responses fits into three major levels: (I) preconventional—a law-obeying, deference stage; (II) conventional—a law-and-order-maintaining stage; and (III) postconventional—a law-creating, principled stage.

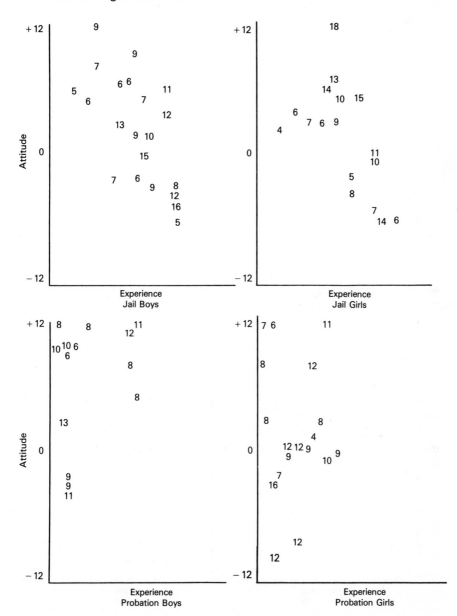

Figure 10-3. Children's Attitude by Experience (age indicated)

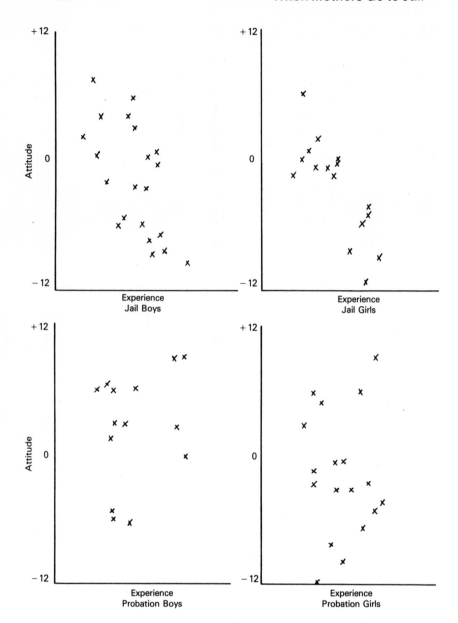

Figure 10-4. Children's Attitude by Experience (residuals)

A series of legal reasoning questions from the Rule-Law Interview developed by Tapp and Levine was used in this study (Appendix J). Since the questions had been used in a U.S. developmental study as well as with children from five other countries including both white and black American samples, there were cross-cultural normative data available. The U.S. Developmental Study was done with children in kindergarten through college plus selected adult groups, including prisoners. Another consideration that favored the use of the Rule-Law Interview was the reported high intercoder reliability (75 to 83 percent).

There was an age difference in the oldest category in the present sample compared to that of Tapp and Levine. Their study included college students in the oldest group, whereas the present study had ages 14 to 18. Both the group of young children (aged 4 to 8) and the middle group (aged 9 to 13) were comparable in age to the schoolchildren studied by Tapp and Levine.

The series of thirteen questions selected from twenty-six in the Rule-Law Interview ranged from simple abstract, such as "what is a law, and why do people obey laws?" to complicated abstract, such as "what does it mean to be right, and what kinds of rights should people have?" These questions were an abrupt departure in tone and content from other questions in the present study and resulted in poor verbal responses. Despite encouragement from the interviewer that only opinions were wanted, the children seemed to approach these questions as if they were a test. After a few unsuccessful attempts to give answers to the easiest questions, some children just gave up. Others continued with difficulty and little enthusiasm.

The difficulties the children had with the questions were somewhat unexpected because the U.S. Developmental Study which was used for comparison purposes included children as young as kindergarteners and reported at least 90 percent codable responses. In the present study the percentage of answers that were codable according to the legal-levels typology averaged 54 percent per question for the children overall.

Some of the difficulty these children had in responding to the questions might be related to their social and academic backgrounds. The comparison sample from Tapp and Levine's study was composed of white subjects drawn from high socioeconomic groups of professional or semiprofessional families. In contrast, the sample of children of offenders was racially mixed and from the lowest socioeconomic levels, in addition to the fact of the mother's criminal status. These children were below average academically and often displayed poor verbal skills. Giving no response or merely saying, "I don't know," seemed to be an easy solution for some of the children when confronted with a difficult question. The questions were presented orally to avoid any difficulties the children might have in reading or writing.

Table 10-3
Children's Legal Reasoning

	Children of Offenders				U.S. Developmental Study		
	4-8 *(31)*	9-13 *(31)*	14-18 *(6)*		K-2 *(20)*	4, 6, 8 *(30)*	College *(65)*
a. What is a law?							
I	32% (10)	64% (18)	50% (1)	I	60%	43%	11%
II	3 (1)	7 (2)	—	II	30	66	71
III	—	—	—	III	—	13	29
DNK	26 (8)	18 (5)	50 (1)				
NC	39 (12)	11 (3)	—				
b. Why should people obey rules/laws?							
I	52% (14)	47% (14)	75% (3)	I	55%	13%	3%
II	—	7 (2)	25 (1)	II	45	66	34
III	—	—	—	III	5	27	56
DNK	18 (5)	27 (8)	—				
NC	30 (8)	20 (6)	—				
c. Why do you obey rules/laws?							
I	62% (16)	70% (19)	80% (4)	I	70%	57%	28%
II	—	4 (1)	20 (1)	II	20	80	46
III	—	—	—	III	—	7	33
DNK	12 (3)	11 (3)	—				
NC	27 (7)	15 (4)	—				
d. Can laws be changed?							
I no	68% (17)	32% (10)	17% (1)	I no	20%	—	—
II } III } yes	20 (5)	26 (8)	67 (4)	II } III } yes	70	100%	95%
DNK	—	13 (4)	—				
NC	12 (3)	29 (9)	—				
e. Are there times when it might be right to break a rule/law?							
I	76% (19)	58% (18)	33% (2)	I	80%	7%	8%
II	12 (3)	19 (6)	67 (4)	II	20	73	35
III	—	—	—	III	—	17	54
DNK	4 (1)	6 (2)	—				
NC	8 (2)	16 (5)	—				
f. What would happen if there were no rules/laws?							
I	75% (21)	80% (20)	83% (5)	I	50%	57%	6%
II	14 (4)	—	—	II	40	84	93
III	—	—	—	III	—	—	8
DNK	7 (2)	13 (4)	17 (1)				
NC	4 (1)	7 (2)	—				

Children of offenders (jail and probation combined) by age, compared with normative groups from U.S. Developmental Study by educational groups.

Source for parts a-f: J.L. Tapp and L. Kohlberg, "Developing Senses of Law and Legal Justice," *Journal of Social Issues* 27 (1971):65-91.

Table 10-3 *(continued)*

Note for parts a-f: Level I = preconventional; Level II = conventional; Level III = postconventional; DNK = does not know; and NC = not codable within legal-levels typology. For the U.S. Developmental Study, all questions except "can rules be changed, and are there times when it might be right to break a rule?" were multiple coded. Therefore percentages may total over 100 percent. Where answers were idiosyncratic or uncodable, the categories were omitted from the table.

		Jail Children	Probation Children	Significance
g. What is a law?				
I	Preconventional	29% (9)	67% (20)	$p < .02$
II	Conventional	3 (1)	7 (2)	
III	Postconventional	—	—	
	Does not know	32 (10)	13 (4)	
	Not codable	36 (11)	13 (4)	
h. What would happen if there were no laws?				
I	Preconventional	67% (22)	90% (28)	$p < .05$
II	Conventional	12 (4)	—	
III	Postconventional	—	—	
	Does not know	12 (4)	10 (3)	
	Not codable	9 (3)	—	

Chi-square (χ^2) tests of statistical significance are used in all tables. N.S. indicates that χ^2 was not significant at the .05 level.

Another explanation for the lower rate of codable responses is that when the children did respond, many of their responses were idiosyncratic. Some responses were highly personalized, usually referring to the mother's illegal conduct. Such responses were occasionally incomprehensible unless some information about the mother's offense was already known. The fact that for all but two of the questions the jail children gave higher percentages of uncodable answers than probation children lends support to the notion that the experience of having a mother in jail contributed somewhat to the personalized quality of the children's responses.

Some responses reflected a differing use of words. For example, in response to the question, "what is a law?" some children replied "a cop" and others "a judge" in reference to their colloquial use of the term *law* to refer to the police and the judiciary.

The nature of the questions limited the ability of the interviewer to coach, probe, or encourage responses by use of examples because of the obvious potential for bias in responses. It was notable that all four of the interviewers expressed dissatisfaction with the rule-law questions, complaining that they were awkward and difficult for the children.

The results obtained using questions from Tapp and Levine's Rule-Law Interview were lower response levels in the present study for all questions across age groups than reported in the U.S. Developmental Study. There was a limited spread of responses and a noticeable absence of level III, postconventional responses. Of the answers that were codable within the three standardized levels, most of the children's responses were preconventional, that is, at the lowest level. For several questions there were numerous "don't know" responses, especially from the younger two groups of children. Questions the children had considerable difficulty with, as reflected by their silence or "don't know" responses were: "what is a fair law; what is a right; and what does it mean to be right?" Due to the low number of codable answers given to these questions, they were omitted from further analysis.

The same form of data analysis as that in the U.S. Developmental Study was used for the sample of jail and probation children combined and divided by age groups. The t-tests for differences between category response percentages for the age levels showed only two significant differences at the $p < .05$ level. The differences were in the expected direction between the middle and older groups for the questions: "are there times when it might be right to break a law?" and "what would you do if someone in charge told you to do something wrong?" Using a chi-square analysis, only one significant difference was found for the question, "can laws be changed?" More conventional answers were given by older children. The two questions for which t-tests indicated differences followed the same trend, though they were not significant according to the chi-square analysis. For both questions, the number of conventional responses of offenders' children increased with age, but none of the children gave postconventional responses.

To the extent that the children's responses did fit the legal-reasoning-levels typology, the results show more lower-level responses than the normative data. For purposes of illustration, two questions are discussed: one which tends to support a developmental progression, the other which contradicts.

In response to the question dealing with the legitimacy of violating a rule/law, "are there times when it might be right to break a law?" the U.S. Developmental Study showed a developmental progression. The majority of the youngest group took both a negative and an absolutist stand against rule breaking. The middle group focused on the morality of the circumstances at the conventional level. The college students responded at the postconventional level. The children of offenders also showed a trend, though not a significant one, of developmental progression in their responses. The percentage of preconventional responses decreased with age. The oldest group gave predominantly conventional answers, with none of the offenders' children espousing postconventional notions of the morality of the law. When the groups are compared, the children of offenders at all ages gave more low-level responses than the normative group (table 10-3e).

In response to the question, "what would happen if there were no laws?" the U.S. Developmental Study reports a marked developmental progression in legal thought from kindergarten through college. In contrast, the majority of the children of offenders at all ages expressed preconventional apprehensions about crime and violence in a world without laws. Although there were no significant differences in their responses by age, the percentage of children expressing preconventional responses *increased* rather than decreased with age, a reversal of the trend observed in the U.S. Developmental Study (table 10-3*f*).

Despite the low-response rates overall, there were significant differences using chi-square analysis between the jail and probation children for two questions. The significant difference in the first question, "what is a law?" can be attributed to the high number of jail children who said they did not know or gave uncodable responses, 32 percent and 36 percent, respectively. In contrast, only 26 percent of the probation children gave either "don't know" or uncodable responses (table 10-3*g*).

The second significant difference between the jail and probation children was in response to the question, "what would happen if there were no laws?" Two-thirds of the jail and almost all the probation children gave preconventional responses, emphasizing the violence and crime that would result if there were no laws. However, 12 percent of the jail but none of the probation children gave conventional responses, suggesting that personal desires would dominate and there would be disorder and chaos (table 10-3*h*).

The children in this study had considerable difficulty responding to the legal-reasoning questions adapted from the Rule-Law Interview. It appears that the questions were not well suited for this population and that the legal-reasoning typology did not gain support from this study.

The hypothesis that jail children would have more exposure with the legal system and express more negative attitudes toward the police than probation children proved inconclusive. Jail children visited mothers in jail, and more jail than probation children witnessed arrests. However, there was no difference in their experienes in court or in their own delinquency. The two groups did not differ significantly in their attitudes toward the police. However, as children had more exposure to the police and the legal system, they developed more negative attitudes toward both. No conclusions can be drawn about the children's legal reasoning.

Discussion

It was anticipated that bad experiences with the police involving one's mother would tend to alienate children from the legal system. Children who witnessed events resulting in negative consequences for their mothers had more negative opinions. Trends indicated that with increased experience with the police, the children expressed more negative attitudes and less confidence in the police.

The children who were interviewed were relatively young and apparently many of them had not formed rigid attitudes toward the police. Interviewers found that children answered their questions about the police in a manner that suggested it was an issue they had never thoughtfully considered before. They rarely expressed any awareness of a relationship between questions about their own or their mother's experiences with the police and questions about their attitudes toward the police. This would suggest that their attitudes were still in the formative stage.

For example, a 7-year-old boy, who had twice been removed from his mother's custody by the police, expressed initial hostility toward the police. In retelling his experiences with the police he made only negative remarks and expressed bitterness about the way the police had treated his mother. He concluded that the police "do awful things and even kill people." The boy related a story in which his mother's boyfriend had beat up his father when he came to visit. Then when asked what adult he would like to be like when he grew older, he promptly replied he wanted to be like the boyfriend. Later in the interview when he was asked what he would like to be, he said he would like to be a "cop." When asked why he wanted to be a "cop", he responded because they had guns and he would like to shoot guns. He then proudly related an experience in which his grandfather had allowed him to shoot a rifle. This experience apparently was more influential in determining his answer to the question than the mother's misfortunes with the police. Perhaps he made little connection between the police who had mistreated his mother and the policeman he could imagine himself to be. This boy, raised almost exclusively by women, showed indications of identifying with heroic male figures. He spoke excitedly about Muhammad Ali and several male television police characters. It is not uncommon for a child to hold contradictory notions without recognizing any apparent conflict.

This child had a similarly ambivalent attitude toward his mother. At one point he related how his mother had mistreated him, and even had old scars from whippings, and yet he still expressed genuine affection for his mother and was considered her favorite of three children. This child seemed to identify positively with those people who were strong enough to defend themselves, such as the boyfriend, the heavyweight boxing champion, and tough television heroes. It suggests that perhaps the mother's mistreatment of this child had actually promoted some admiration for strong dominant figures, including the police.

A number of the children's interviews revealed similarly complex and contradictory attitudes. Older children's attitudes about the police were more negatively affected by their experiences with the police than were younger children as shown by their negative impressions about the police and their increasing reluctance with age to report criminal incidents.

It is not possible to determine on the basis of these interviews what future attitudes these children will develop. What can be said with some assurance is that these attitudes will not be formed solely on the basis of a few bad experiences with the police. As they grow older, the children will become increasingly aware of the negative attitudes of an influential subculture in their communities. It is likely that a child's upbringing and cumulative experience are more influential in the long run than any single experience, good or bad.

11 Child's Performance in School

Analysis

An effort was made to investigate whether the confinement of a mother in jail affected a child's behavior outside the family circle. Since the study dealt with children aged 4 to 18, school was an outside institution in which almost all would be involved. This study examined the hypothesis that jail children compared to probation children would perform less satisfactorily in school. The question of whether a mother's incarceration has any discernible influence on her child in school is, of course, subject to serious methodological problems in a short-term study. The question that could be directly addressed was whether children whose mothers were inmates differed in their school behavior and performance from children whose mothers were on probation.

Although very little research has been done concerning how children are affected by incarceration of parents, a study by Friedman and Esselstyn (1965) looked at school performances of children of fathers imprisoned at Elmwood Rehabilitation Center of Santa Clara County. (Women in Elmwood were included in the present study.) Their study compared children of male inmates in kindergarten through seventh grade with classmates; 73 percent of the sample were boys. The groups were not compared socioeconomically, and the authors point out there was an overrepresentation of Mexican-Americans in the jail population. They found that sons of jail inmates were rated by teachers as below average in school on social and psychological characteristics more frequently than classmates in the control groups. Although specific data were not given and the design would not justify drawing causal connections, the authors conclude with the implication that committing a father to jail is soon accompanied by a decline in the school performance of his children.

Some of the shortcomings in the Friedman and Esselstyn study are avoided in the present study: boys and girls were included in approximately equal numbers and there was an ethnic mix. Socioeconomic status and the mother's prior criminal record were taken into account. The comparison group was children of mothers on probation.

The majority of the children in the present study were enrolled in school as would be expected due to their ages. In California, children are eligible to begin school when they are 4 years and 9 months old. School attendance

89

becomes compulsory at age 6. Despite the fact that all the children qualified for school, some were not enrolled. From the mothers' reports, 12 percent of the jail and 6 percent of the probation children were not in school. There were teenagers who had dropped out of school, reputedly because of lack of interest, repeated expulsion, and in one case, pregnancy. In a few cases, young children were not attending school because mothers reportedly felt school was not necessary yet. In one instance a jail mother, Linda R., mentioned difficulty properly dressing her 6-year-old daughter, Felicia, for school because of the expense. Consequently, Felicia had not attended school regularly the previous year and was currently repeating first grade. The school principal confirmed that the mother put great emphasis on having her child well-dressed for school and mentioned that because of derogatory remarks made about the family by a welfare worker, the mother had returned a bag of clothing intended for the child. According to the principal, Felicia's attendance had been so infrequent after this incident with the welfare worker the school did not qualify for federal funds based on the child's attendance and consequently she was not considered enrolled.

According to the mothers' reports about children in school, 71 percent of the jail and 78 percent of the probation children were in elementary school, that is, sixth grade or lower. The rest of the children were in junior or senior high school (table 11-1*a*).

The children were interviewed about their attitudes toward school. When asked for a self-report about how they were doing in school, there were no significant differences in the replies of the two groups. Most of the children gave unelaborated remarks, such as "okay," "good," and "fine" (table 11-1*b*). Likewise, when asked how they felt about school, most gave simple, favorable responses about liking school (table 11-1*c*). Even children who were verbose during the rest of the interview, tended to give brief responses to questions about school. The brevity of the responses could have been due to the routine nature of the questions and that children learn early to give acceptable, noncontroversial replies on some topics. The questioning of the children about their feelings did not yield much useful information. There was no differentiation between the jail and probation children, both groups gave superficial remarks and mostly noncritical appraisals about school.

Efforts were made to obtain ongoing information about the children from school records. The research problems encountered in this effort account for the discontinuous nature of the information that was available for most of the children. Delays in access to school records contributed to the difficulty in obtaining information and the lack of information in the school files compounded the problem. The fact that 40 percent of the children for whom school information could be obtained were in the earliest grades meant that the children had no prior established school record on which to base comparisons. Additionally, many children changed schools one or more times after the mother went to jail. In the case of one boy in

Table 11-1
Children in School

	Jail Children	Probation Children	Significance
a. Mother's report of child's grade in school			
K-1st	16% (5)	23% (8)	N.S.
2d	28 (9)	11 (4)	
3d	9 (3)	9 (3)	
4th	9 (3)	17 (6)	
5th	6 (2)	9 (3)	
6th	6 (2)	17 (6)	
7th	6 (2)	6 (2)	
8th	3 (1)	6 (2)	
9th +	16 (5)	3 (1)	
b. Child's report about how he is doing in school			
Poorly	14% (4)	12% (4)	N.S.
Average, okay	38 (11)	46 (15)	
Fine, good	48 (14)	42 (14)	
c. Child reports whether he likes school			
No	19% (6)	6% (2)	N.S.
Mixed	16 (5)	15 (5)	
Yes	65 (20)	79 (27)	
d. Child's school behavior as reported by teacher			
Poor, below average	50% (11)	22% (4)	N.S.
Normal, average	41 (9)	50 (9)	
Excellent	9 (2)	28 (5)	
e. Self-esteem rating by teacher or counselor			
Low self-esteem	57% (13)	22% (4)	N.S.
Average	17 (4)	33 (6)	
High	20 (5)	44 (8)	
Not know child well	4 (1)	—	
f. Child's academic performance			
Low, below average	70% (16)	17% (3)	$p < .01$
Average, grade level	26 (6)	50 (9)	
High, above average	4 (1)	33 (6)	

Chi-square (x^2) tests of statistical significance are used in all tables. N.S. indicates that x^2 was not significant at the .05 level.

junior high school, by the time approval had been granted to review the child's records, he had already transferred schools. Previous records of transfer students were often unavailable. Teacher's cited poor attendance as the reason some children did not have standard test scores. Attendance records showed 39 percent of the jail and 17 percent of the probation children had frequent absences from school.

Teachers were better sources of information about how children were doing in school than were the children's own remarks. There was variability in the teachers' ability and willingness to comment on the children. Laws concerning confidentiality of school records and student and parent access to such records were a concern of some principals and teachers. A few remarked that they preferred to discuss the students rather than write reports. Observations made by school personnel were frequently copious, but not easily subject to categorization or quantification. Teachers tended to notice and discuss extremes in the children's adjustment rather than minor variations in behavior or academic performance. There was not a consistent pattern in the changes in children's behavior perceived by the teachers. There were more anecdotal remarks about jail than probation children. Some described children whose behavior improved dramatically when the mother went to jail and others told about children whose behavior deteriorated.

In the M— family, the mother was a heroin addict convicted of welfare fraud. Her two children, Gwen aged 7 and Monte aged 8, apparently flourished in school during their mother's absence. They had moved in with their uncle who made a daily practice of driving the children back to their own neighborhood school. The teachers who were interviewed did not realize the mother was in jail, but assumed she was out of town or in a drug program. Both the teachers and the principal commented upon the striking improvements in the children. Their attendance changed from poor to regular, their appearance and clothes were cleaner, and one teacher noted that Monte had begun to socialize with his classmates. In the past, these children would sometimes arrive at school in the middle of the day looking disoriented, dirty, ill-clothed, and hungry. One of the teachers had unwittingly remarked to Gwen that she hoped her mother would stay wherever she was because Gwen was doing so much better while she was gone.

On the other hand, some teachers reported jail children who had become more easily distracted and moody in class when their mother was away. Others reported children being sullen and still others more aggressive and with occasional tantrums.

Teachers' reports of the children's school behavior indicate that half of the jail children had poor classroom behavior and were disciplinary problems compared to 22 percent of the probation children. Several children were identified as "regular troublemakers" who frequently were disruptive in class. Although there was not a significant difference in the reported behavior of the two groups, the obvious trend was that more jail children were behaving unsatisfactorily at school (table 11-1d).

In an effort to standardize the teachers' comments about the children, they were asked to complete a Behavior Rating Form (Coopersmith, 1967; Appendix G). This instrument included items for evaluating the self-esteem of children, the questions were relevant for school-aged children, and it was easily administered. It refers to such behaviors as the child's reactions to failure, self-confidence in a new situation, sociability with peers, and the need for encouragement and reassurance. According to Coopersmith, on the basis of theoretical and empirical grounds, the behaviors measured were assumed to be an external manifestation of the child's self-esteem. A scale rating system summarizing the children's scores was used, and the children were then ranked according to whether they had high, medium, or low self-esteem. The difference between the two groups was not significant, but the trend was for the jail children to have lower scores, with over half of them in the lowest category (table 11-1e).

The most objective measures obtained were the records of the children's academic performance. Although the means of evaluating academic performance differed from school to school and from grade to grade, all schools made efforts to evaluate their pupils. Because of the diversity of academic measures used by the schools, rank within a class was chosen as the measure by which to compare the children. On the basis of class standing as a measure of academic performance, there was a significant difference between the two groups of children. The jail children were performing at low or below average levels in disproportionate numbers compared to the probation group: 70 percent of the jail compared to 17 percent of the probation children were below average, or in the bottom third of their class. Even more revealing, far fewer of the jail children were doing well as indicated by being in the top third of the class: 4 percent of the jail compared to 33 percent of the probation children (table 11-1f). The statistically significant difference between the two groups of children in terms of their academic performance supports the hypothesis that jail children would perform less satisfactorily in school.

An analysis was done to see if there was still a significant finding after the mother's prior criminal record and socioeconomic status were partialed out. The mother's prior record and socioeconomic status together accounted for 40 percent of the variance in academic performance, whereas the mother's current legal status accounted for only 8 percent of the variance. It therefore appears that the long-term factors of socioeconomic status and mother's criminal record were more influential in causing the observed difference between the children's academic performance than whether or not the mother was currently in jail.

In this section, the child's behavior and performance in the school environment were explored by questioning the children, interviewing the teachers, and reviewing the children's school records. No distinguishing information was obtained from the children themselves due to their brief, superficial comments about school. The teachers' remarks tended to emphasize noticeable extremes in the jail children's behavior. The behavior rating forms that were used in an effort to standardize the teachers' appraisal of the children's self-esteem did not indicate a significant difference, but the jail children tended to be rated lower than the probation children. The school records of the children's academic performance did reveal a significant difference between the two groups, with the jail children performing less well. The significant difference in the children's academic performance, as well as the trends indicating that the jail children had more behavioral problems and lower self-esteem, support the hypothesis that jail children perform less satisfactorily in school than probation children. Further analysis indicated that the difference in academic performance between the two groups of children could be better accounted for by the mother's prior criminal record and the family's socioeconomic status than by the mother's temporary status in jail or on probation.

Discussion

In the analysis of this study, measures of children's behavior in school were dependent on academic records and teachers' evaluations. Some general observations based on background information of the children can enhance an understanding of their school performance.

Although the study found that jail children were performing less well than their classmates, this poor performance cannot be attributed solely to the mother's incarceration. An analysis of the mother's socioeconomic status and prior criminal record was found to be more influential in determining a child's academic performance than the fact the mother was currently in jail. Understandably, long-term factors such as poverty, low status, and a mother's criminal record would be more detrimental to a child than a temporary circumstance.

Most children were found to continue behavior patterns which had been established prior to their mother's current incarceration. Teachers were often unable to distinguish the child's behavior before and during the mother's absence. Most of the behavioral problems and low self-esteem children displayed were long-standing. Teachers often were unaware of domestic problems due to poor communication or no contact between the school and family. In specific cases teachers were able to identify some noticeable change in a child's behavior and attendance during the mother's incarceration. These changes were sometimes detrimental but occasionally they were not.

The most interesting case in which behavior and attendance improved occurred in the M— family. Based on the mother's and children's descriptions, their household before the arrest could be described as unstable, even chaotic. The mother, an addict, had recently broken up with her boyfriend, and the conflict and tension which preceded the actual breakdown of that relationship had further disrupted their lives. The mother did not make a practice of waking or feeding her children and sending them to school. Some mornings she was not home but more typically she slept until midday. She reported never having attended a school function or meeting a teacher. Upon her arrest, her two grade-school-aged children went to live with their unemployed uncle. The uncle displayed genuine affection and concern for his niece and nephew. He took responsibility for the children and made them feel they were part of a cohesive household. He assigned jobs to each child, drove them to and from school, and took an interest in their schoolwork. With these changes the children found themselves living in quite different circumstances. Despite the fact they were still living in an impoverished neighborhood, their uncle exhibited a strong sense of pride in himself and his household. He brought a sense of order, stability, and affection to the children and gave them a feeling of belonging and contributing to the household. It is interesting to note how quickly subtantial changes appeared in the children's attitudes and behavior both in school and out, brought about by this shift of supervision.

More commonly a child's daily routine was disrupted when the mother went to jail. Three kinds of discontinuity children commonly experienced were changes of caretaker, household, and school. Children who began to have problems in school typically were found to have experienced at least two of these disruptions. There appeared to be less upset when the child remained at home and the caretaker was a close relative or someone the child had known before. However, when a child changed households and schools, he had to contend with new daily routines both at home and school.

The study found that although changes were disruptive to a child, it was the quality of the change that was critical. When a child went from an established routine to a less stable situation, his schoolwork never improved. In the M— family the children experienced a change in caretaker and a change in household and yet their situation was such an obvious improvement in terms of attention, affection, and stability that this disruption brought about improvement in school performance. In other words, changes which resulted in a more stable and secure home situation were usually beneficial for the child. Disruptions which created more uncertainty for the child were likely to produce either no noticeable change or a possible decline in school performance.

12 Welfare Status of Child

Analysis

In arguments against imprisonment of criminal offenders, some social commentators suggest one of the costs of incarcerating parents is that their children become burdens on the welfare system. Characteristically, Burkhart, citing the American Association of University Women study (1969) in which it was estimated that 80 percent of convicted mothers supported children, suggested that the incarceration of mothers "created its own welfare recipients" (Burkhart, 1971). All too often, economic arguments such as this are put forward in an unqualified and unquestioned manner.

This study tested the hypothesis that more jail than probation children would become welfare recipients as a consequence of their mothers' sentence. The results of the study showed a slight decline in the number of children in both groups who were receiving welfare following a mother's arrest. While the number of jail children on welfare remained approximately the same during the mother's incarceration, there was a slight decline at the time of the follow-up interviews approximately one month after the mother's release. There was a substantial decline in the number of probation children dependent on welfare assistance during the course of the mother's probation.

An important factor to consider in assessing whether incarceration increases welfare dependence is that most of the children whose mothers were jailed were already on welfare before their mothers were arrested. Based on information obtained for the entire sample at the time of the first interview, 76 percent of the jail and 83 percent of the probation children were receiving welfare assistance, usually in the form of Aid to Families with Dependent Children (AFDC), at the time of the mother's arrest (table 12-1*a*).

At time I, while the mothers were serving their sentences, the number of children receiving welfare declined slightly in both groups, but 72 percent of the jail and 73 percent of the probation children continued to receive assistance (table 12-1*b*).

An example of a child who retained welfare status when the mother went to jail is Josie T. Her mother had been receiving AFDC benefits and supplemented her income by prostitution. Upon the mother's arrest, Josie, 10, went to live with the mother's sister who took over responsibility for her

Table 12-1
Financial Support of Child

		Jail Children (118)	Probation Children (48)	Significance
a.	Child's source of financial support before mother's sentence (time 0)[a]			N.S.
	Mother alone	8% (10)	4% (2)	
	Welfare	76 (90)	83 (40)	
	Grandparents	1 (1)	—	
	Other	14 (17)	12 (6)	
b.	Child's source of financial support after mother's arrest (time 1)[a]			$p < .01$
	Mother alone	—	7% (3)	
	Welfare	72% (85)	78 (35)	
	Grandparents	10 (12)	—	
	Other	18 (21)	16 (7)	

		Jail Children (52)	Probation Children (44)	Significance
c.	Mother's report if child being supported by welfare assistance (mothers who were interviewed twice)[b]			
	Time 0: before arrest			N.S.
	Yes	88% (46)	86% (38)	
	No	12 (6)	14 (6)	
	Time I: during sentence			N.S.
	Yes	88 (46)	77 (34)	
	No	12 (6)	23 (10)	
	Time II: after release			$p < .005$
	Yes	81 (42)	48 (21)	
	No	19 (10)	52 (23)	

		Jail Mothers (54)	Probation Mothers (21)	Significance
d.	Family received welfare when mother was a child			$p < .02$
	Yes	30% (16)	10% (2)	
	No	52 (28)	90 (19)	
	Does not know	4 (2)	—	
	Missing	15 (8)	—	
e.	Has mother ever received welfare assistance as an adult?			N.S.
	Yes	89% (48)	95% (20)	
	No	7 (4)	5 (1)	
	Missing	4 (2)	—	

[a]Based on responses from all mothers at first interview.

[b]Based only on responses from mothers who were interviewed twice.

Chi-square (x^2) tests of statistical significance are used in all tables. N.S. indicates that x^2 was not significant at the .05 level.

care while the mother was in jail. The aunt quickly became Josie's legal guardian in order to be eligible to receive AFDC payments for Josie. Consequently, Josie's welfare status continued without interruption. This situation was typical for over half of the jail children in this study.

Since many of the children lived in families in which the mother was the head of household, there was necessarily some shifting of responsibility for a child's care when the mother was incarcerated. This shift did not always involve beginning or discontinuing welfare benefits. For example, though none of the jail children continued to be supported by the mother exclusively when she went to jail, most of these children were taken care of financially by grandparents or others without becoming dependent on welfare assistance.

It is apparent that the welfare status of the majority of the children in this study antedated the mother's arrest. The data indicate that a majority of the children in this environment were supported by welfare payments at a poverty level of subsistence. With more than three out of four children in this study being supported by government assistance, this group could be characterized as part of the welfare class before any arrest occurs. This finding refutes the notion that the arrest and incarceration of mothers forces their children onto the welfare rolls.

A more complete analysis of the source of financial support for the children came from the mothers who were interviewed twice and reported information about their financial status before arrest, during incarceration, and after release. Based on these reports, 88 percent of the jail children were on welfare at the time of their mother's arrest and there was no change in this number while the mothers were in jail. After the mothers' release there was a slight decline to 81 percent of the jail children who remained on welfare at time II (table 12-1c).

A more marked decline in the number of children on welfare occurred for the probation children, from 86 percent at the time of the mother's arrest to 77 percent at the time of the first interview and then down to 48 percent at time II. It should be understood that it was good strategy for a woman to find a job before her sentencing because of the positive, industrious impression this would create for the judge. Mothers who were not detained had a greater opportunity to retain or locate jobs and thus were more likely to be put on probation with no jail time. More importantly, once a woman was on probation, she remained in the community and was often encouraged by her probation officer to find a job. On occasion probation officers were helpful in assisting women to find jobs. In contrast, the jailed mother had no such opportunities to retain or find a job by which she could support her children.

Lucille L. was a fairly typical example of a mother sentenced to probation. She had a low-paying job as a housekeeper and was receiving welfare before her arrest. She was convicted of welfare fraud for receiving higher AFDC payments than she was entitled to legitimately. Conditions of her probation were that she make restitution for the excess money she had received and that she become more financially responsible. Her probation officer helped her find a new job earning the minimum wage in a laundry and helped her cut expenses by finding cheaper living accommodations. She was then able to live on her earnings and her child no longer received welfare support. She also made a gesture toward paying restitution to the county.

Women with sentences of probation could continue to receive welfare payments. In fact, based on the interviews at time I, most of the probation mothers continued to receive some form of government assistance: 83 percent of the probation children had been supported by welfare money at the time of arrest and 73 percent continued to be supported by welfare assistance at time I. Pressure exerted by probation officers to become self-sufficient presumably contributed to the decline in numbers of mothers dependent on welfare. Some probation mothers reported feeling they would be better off and less vulnerable to criminal involvement if they had nothing to do with the welfare system. A young mother when interviewed expressed the frustration of many about continuing on welfare, saying, "I wanted to get off welfare, didn't want no part of it. It's what got me into all this trouble. I'm better off without the welfare people and all their rules and regulations."

Previously employed jail mothers, on the other hand, were unable to continue supporting their children while they were incarcerated. Only 8 percent of the jail children had been solely supported by their mothers prior to her arrest, and this, of course, ceased in all cases when the mother went to jail.

Some shifting of the jail children's financial support occurred as they acquired new caretakers. Some children went off welfare, but this number was displaced by others who went on welfare, so the overall percentage of jail children on welfare remained constant.

A comon occurrence for jail children was to be cared for by grand-parents who, in some cases, also assumed financial responsibility. Only 1 percent of the jail children had been supported by grandparents before the mother's arrest. Afterward, this number increased to 10 percent during the period of incarceration. Some children lived with grandparents who were already receiving welfare so their status did not change (tables 12-1a and b).

A national survey of women's correctional programs conducted by Glick and Neto (1977) is in accordance with the findings of this study. Although the national data indicate that over half (55.6 percent) of the female inmates had received welfare, there were differences in the percentages receiving welfare from state to state. It was suggested these differences were related more to welfare policies than to the actual economic needs or status of the individual. In California, 70.6 percent of incarcerated women had been receiving welfare, with a higher percentage of blacks (73.8 percent) than for whites (66.6 percent). Women with greater numbers of children were more likely to be recipients of welfare, since most qualified for programs designated to aid dependent children rather than for themselves. The four county jails in this study were also in the national survey, and the mothers had a greater dependence on welfare than the state average for incarcerated women.

Among jail mothers there appeared to be widespread and ongoing dependency on government assistance. Jail sentences did not appear to be responsible for either creating or breaking this dependency. Sentencing mothers to jail did not force large numbers of children onto welfare rolls or create a new group of welfare recipients. The fact that incarceration did not have much impact on the financial support of these children was because they were already part of a larger welfare class. Almost a third of the jail mothers had received welfare when they were children, and as adults 89 percent had received welfare at some time (table 12-1d and e). Not unexpectedly, even their children showed signs of continuing this pattern of dependency on government support. The case of one jail child, Malinda A., a black, unwed, pregnant 15-year-old girl illustrates this legacy of dependency. She reported she was looking forward to the birth of her child so she could move out of her mother's house and into an apartment to establish her own household supported by welfare. Although the mother did not want her teen-aged daughter to move out, she pointed out that a separate household arrangement would maximize the amount of financial and housing assistance they would be eligible to receive.

In summary, the hypothesis that more jail than probation children would become welfare recipients as a consequence of their mothers' sentence was not supported by this study. However, more jail than probation children remained welfare recipients after their mothers were sentenced. Probation appears to have been effective in getting some of the women off welfare, at least in the short period covered by this study.

The data from this study and the national survey data support the widely held perception that incarceration is related to poverty and social class. It suggests that fundamental changes are required to eradicate the high reliance on welfare assistance that exists among convicted women.

Discussion

A dependence on some form of government assistance was commonplace in the communities in which these women lived. During preliminary interviews some women in jail did not acknowledge being on welfare. This appeared not to be a matter of deception or embarrassment since they would readily acknowledge receiving specific forms of government assistance, such as AFDC, food stamps, and general assistance. Mothers in jail would commonly make the distinction that they themselves were not on welfare but their children were supported by AFDC. Consequently, it was necessary to adjust the questionnaires to accommodate this need for specificity.

A few women, especially those arrested for welfare fraud, expressed a desire to become financially self-sufficient. Their motivation appeared to be an effort to eliminate interference in their lives by social workers and the risk of punishment due to conviction of welfare fraud. At the time of the follow-up interview there was little indication that these women would be successful in this endeavor.

The majority of the women did not speak of eliminating the need for welfare support in the near future. They appeared to accept welfare assistance as a way of life, in many cases having received it as children. Their children often had known no other form of support. It would be unrealistic to ignore the fact that children, aware of their welfare status, will in time come to accept this definition of themselves.

13 After Mother's Release from Jail

Analysis

So far, the previous hypotheses have dealt primarily with the period of incarceration and events leading up to incarceration. These topics were explored in interviews with the mothers and children while the mother was in jail (referred to as time I interviews). Also of interest and concern is what happens to these mothers and their children after the mother is released from jail. To examine this issue, a second set of interviews (time II interviews) was designed to explore the circumstances of mothers and children after release. Time II interviews took place in the mothers' homes approximately one month after release.

It was hypothesized that most jail mothers and their children would be reunited after the mother's release from jail, though no previous study was found that had done follow-up research to support this expectation. Interest extended beyond the issue of whether or not mothers and children were reunited, and an attempt was made to evaluate the adjustment of both mothers and children.

A major problem in the pursuit of data for this hypothesis was actually locating the mothers after their release for time II interviews. Some jail mothers left town immediately after release, others changed their names, still others were in flight from the law, and a few were back in jail. In contrast, all probation mothers were easily located and cooperated in follow-up interviews.

The "lost" and the followed-up mothers were compared on the basis of demographic characteristics and experiential information obtained at the time I interview. They were statistically comparable on all these indexes; that is, no factor distinguished the groups or was related to the attrition (table 13-1). A comparison was also made of jail and probation children who were seen for both time I and II interviews with children who had been interviewed only once. There were no significant differences between jail children who had been successfully followed up and those who had been seen only once (table 13-2). Three probation children were interviewed only once and they were not significantly different from those who were interviewed twice; the three children were unrepresentative only because they realized their mother was on probation.

Table 13-1

Comparison of Lost and Followed-up Jail Mothers

(jail mothers—54)

	Followed up (27)	Lost (27)		Followed up (27)	Lost (27)
Age		N.S.	**Racial group**		N.S.
18-25	37% (10)	37% (10)	White	26% (7)	37% (10)
26-30	37 (10)	30 (8)	Black	52 (14)	44 (12)
31-40	26 (7)	30 (8)	Mex-Amer	15 (4)	15 (4)
41-50	—	4 (1)	Nat-Amer/other	7 (2)	4 (1)
Education		N.S.	**Employed**		N.S.
College	11% (3)	22% (6)	Yes	26% (7)	41% (11)
High school	30 (8)	22 (6)	No	74 (20)	59 (16)
Some H.S.	41 (11)	37 (10)			
9th grade	18 (5)	18 (5)			
On welfare		N.S.	**Marital status**		N.S.
Yes	74% (20)	63% (17)	Married	26% (7)	33% (9)
No	26 (7)	37 (10)	Common law	15 (4)	18 (5)
			Sep/Divorced	30 (8)	30 (8)
			Widowed	4 (1)	4 (1)
			Single	26 (7)	15 (4)
Prior living arrangement		N.S.	**No. of dependents**		N.S.
W/child alone	37% (10)	37% (10)	1	7% (2)	11% (3)
W/child and husband	4 (1)	30 (8)	2	30 (8)	30 (8)
W/child and boyfriend	26 (7)	15 (4)	3	26 (7)	11 (3)
W/child and grandparent	15 (4)	7 (2)	4	18 (5)	30 (8)
W/child and relatives	7 (2)	7 (2)	5	4 (1)	4 (1)
W/child and other	11 (3)	4 (1)	6	4 (1)	11 (3)
			7	7 (2)	—
			8	4 (1)	4 (1)
Probation		N.S.	**Drug-related offense**		N.S.
Never	52% (14)	48% (13)	No	33% (9)	56% (15)
Past violation	7 (2)	19 (5)	Yes, drug	52 (14)	22 (6)
Current violation	41 (11)	33 (9)	Yes, alcohol	15 (4)	15 (4)
			Indirectly	—	7 (2)
Sentence		N.S.	**Drug use**		N.S.
30 days	7% (2)	18% (5)	Nonuser	22% (6)	37% (10)
30-90 days	52 (14)	26 (7)	Drug user	22 (6)	11 (3)
90 days to 6 mos.	15 (4)	33 (9)	Drug addict	33 (9)	33 (9)
6 mos.-1 yr.	22 (6)	15 (4)	Alcoholic	18 (5)	11 (3)
1 year	4 (1)	7 (2)	Drugs and alcohol	4 (1)	7 (2)

Table 13-1 (*cont.*)

	Followed up (27)	Lost (27)		Followed up (27)	Lost (27)
Length of residence		N.S.	Socioeconomic status		N.S.
< 1 year	41% (11)	48% (13)	II-III	4% (1)	11% (3)
> 1 year	59 (16)	52 (14)	IV	11 (3)	15 (4)
			V (lowest)	85 (23)	74 (20)
			Arrested or		
Prior arrests		N.S.	surrendered		N.S.
No	41% (11)	41% (11)	Arrested	96% (26)	82% (22)
Yes	59 (16)	59 (16)	Surrendered	4 (1)	18 (5)
			Detained at time		
Offense category		N.S.	of arrest		N.S.
Property	41% (11)	59% (16)	Yes	89% (24)	85% (22)
Violent	22 (6)	22 (6)	No	11 (3)	15 (4)
Narcotics	37 (10)	15 (4)			
Other	—	4 (1)	Caretaker during		
			mother's incar-		
Mother's post-			ceration		N.S.
release plans		N.S.	Nuclear family	15% (4)	22% (6)
W/child	63% (17)	44% (12)	Grandparents	48 (13)	44 (12)
W/child,			Other relative	26 (7)	4 (1)
no plans	22 (6)	30 (8)	Foster care	4 (1)	11 (3)
Not W/child	11 (3)	18 (5)	Other	7 (2)	15 (4)
No plans	4 (1)	7 (2)	Self	—	4 (1)
Mother's ex-					
pected problem		N.S.	County		N.S.
Child	22% (6)	15% (4)	Alameda	33% (9)	18% (5)
Place to live	26 (7)	33 (9)	San Francisco	41 (11)	22 (6)
Financial	26 (7)	18 (5)	San Mateo	11 (3)	15 (4)
Other	4 (1)	22 (6)	Santa Clara	15 (4)	44 (12)
Drugs/alcohol	22 (6)	7 (2)			
No problem	—	4 (1)			

Chi-square (χ^2) tests of statistical significance are used in all tables. N.S. indicates that χ^2 was not significant at the .05 level.

The following discussion deals only with mothers and children interviewed at time II. As predicted by the hypothesis, most of the jail children (75 percent) were reunited with their mothers after their release from jail. One-fourth of the jail children were not living with their mothers at time II, approximately one month after the mother's release (table 13-3a). The reasons for the continued separation included a husband who refused to relinquish the child and had begun divorce proceedings, an unmarried

Table 13-2
Comparison of Interviewed Children Who Were Followed up and Children Seen at Time I or II only

	Jail Children (49)		Probation Children (35)	
	Followed up (29)	I or II Only (20)	Followed up (32)	I or II Only (3)
Age		N.S.		N.S.
4-8	45%(13)	50%(10)	41%(13)	33%(1)
9-13	34 (10)	30 (6)	56 (18)	33 (1)
14-18	21 (6)	20 (4)	3 (1)	33 (1)
Sex		N.S.		N.S.
Boy	55%(16)	55%(11)	44%(14)	33%(1)
Girl	45 (13)	45 (9)	56 (18)	67 (2)
Racial group / Child's ethnicity		N.S.		N.S.
White	21% (6)	11% (2)	53%(17)	33%(1)
Black	65 (19)	84 (16)	44 (14)	67 (2)
Mex-Amer	14 (4)	5 (1)	3 (1)	—
Child knows mother in jail / Child knows mother on prob.		N.S.		N.S.
Yes	83%(24)	90%(17)	36%(10)	100%(3)
No	3 (1)	5 (1)	57 (16)	—
Uncertain	14 (4)	5 (1)	7 (2)	—
Child present at mother's arrest		N.S.		N.S.
Yes, present	45%(13)	21%(4)	22%(6)	—
Not present, but remembers	10 (3)	16 (3)	11 (3)	100%(3)
Not present, not remember	31 (9)	53 (10)	7 (2)	—
Child not aware	14 (4)	10 (2)	59 (16)	—

Child's understanding of why mother was arrested

		N.S.
Knows offense	65% (19)	44% (8)
Knows broke law, unclear about offense	7 (2)	22 (4)
Not understand	14 (4)	22 (4)
Not aware	14 (4)	11 (2)

Change of school since mother's arrest

		N.S.
No	45% (13)	32% (6)
Yes	38 (11)	52 (10)
Does not apply, not in school	17 (5)	16 (3)

Caretaker during mother's sentence

		N.S.
Grandparents	38% (11)	16% (3)
Self/sibling	10 (3)	10.5 (2)
"Father"	10 (3)	10.5 (2)
Other relative	14 (4)	37 (7)
Foster care	7 (2)	16 (3)
Other	21 (6)	10.5 (2)

Child's understanding of why mother was arrested

		N.S.
Knows offense	35% (10)	67% (2)
Knows broke law, unclear about offense	3 (1)	33 (1)
Not understand	3 (1)	—
Not aware	59 (17)	—

Change of school since mother's arrest

		N.S.
No	69% (20)	100% (3)
Yes	28 (8)	—
Does not apply, not in school	3 (1)	—

Not applicable; all children living with mothers

Chi-square (χ^2) tests of statistical significance are used in all tables. N.S. indicates that χ^2 was not significant at the .05 level.

Table 13-3
After Release, Time II

	Jail Mothers by Child (53)	Probation Mothers by Child (47)	Significance
a. Is child living with mother at time II, after release			
Yes	75%(38)	100%(47)	$p < .02$
No, with grandparents	10 (5)	—	
No, with father	6 (3)	—	
No, other relative	4 (2)	—	
No, foster care	4 (2)	—	
No, other	2 (1)	—	
b. Does child know about mother's sentence			
Yes	89%(47)	53%(25)	$p < .001$
No	9 (5)	40 (19)	
Mother does not know	2 (1)	—	
c. Mother's report whether child asks about her sentence			
Yes	55%(29)	26%(12)	$p < .001$
No	32 (17)	28 (13)	
Child does not know	6 (3)	40 (19)	
Missing	8 (4)	6 (3)	
d. Child's response when asked about mother's situation	*Jail children (36)*		
Truth, in jail	17%(6)		
Another story	36 (13)		
"I don't know"	17 (6)		
Nothing	11 (4)		
Not asked	19 (7)		

	Jail Mothers (27)	Probation Mothers (21)	Significance
e. Is mother living in same residence as before			
Yes, same	33%(9)	76%(16)	$p < .01$
No, different	63 (17)	19 (4)	
Mother in jail	4 (1)	—	
f. Whom is mother living with			
Child alone	22%(6)	48%(10)	$p < .02$
Child and grandparents	22 (6)	14 (3)	
Child and adult male	11 (3)	38 (8)	
Child and others	15 (4)	—	
Parents w/o child	4 (1)	—	
Other	22 (6)	—	
Alone	4 (1)	—	

Table 13-3 *(continued)*

	Jail Mothers by Child (27)	Probation Mothers by Child (21)	Significance
g. Mother describes jail/ probation to child (by mother)			
Negative	33%(9)	5%(1)	*p* < .005
Tolerable	22 (6)	10 (2)	
Positive	—	5 (1)	
Other	15 (4)	—	
Mother does not talk about it	7 (2)	—	
Child does not know	11 (3)	48 (10)	
Missing	11 (3)	33 (7)	
h. Does child tell others about mother's criminal status (by mother)			
No	44%(12)	14%(3)	*p* < .001
Yes, mother dislikes	11 (3)	—	
Yes, mother not mind	18 (5)	—	
Mother does not know	15 (4)	10 (2)	
Child does not know	11 (3)	48 (10)	
Missing	—	29 (6)	
i. Mother's report of child's behavior toward her since release (by mother)			
Same	59%(16)		
Worse	30 (8)		
Better	—		
Does not apply	11 (3)		
j. Mother's report of child's general behavior			
No change	44%(12)	71%(15)	N.S.
Worse	26 (7)	29 (6)	
Better	11 (3)	—	
Mother does not know	19 (5)	—	
k. Mother's report whether child has been in trouble with police, etc.			
No	52%(14)	62%(13)	N.S.
Yes	37 (10)	19 (4)	
Missing	11 (3)	19 (4)	
l. Is mother employed			
Yes, same job	4%(1)	19%(4)	N.S.
Yes, different job	7 (2)	24 (5)	
No, looking for job	33 (9)	24 (5)	
No, not looking	56 (15)	33 (7)	

Table 13-3 *(continued)*

	Jail Mothers (27)	Probation Mothers (21)	Significance
m. Mother's present job			
Semiprofessional, technicians	—	5%(1)	N.S.
Skilled workers, craftsmen	—	5 (1)	
Clerical workers	7%(2)	14 (3)	
Sales workers	—	5 (1)	
Semiskilled workers	—	5 (1)	
Personal services	4 (1)	5 (1)	
Unemployed	89 (24)	57 (12)	
(1 is in jail)			
n. Mother's anticipated problems upon release (time I)			
Getting settled	33%(9)		
Getting job, financial	19 (5)		
With child	15 (4)		
Marital	4 (1)		
Other	22 (6)		
No problem	7 (2)		
o. Mother's reported problems at time II			
Getting settled	37%(10)	—	$p < .005$
Financial, finding job	41 (11)	19% (4)	
With child	—	5 (1)	
Other	4 (1)	5 (1)	
No problems	11 (3)	52 (11)	
Missing	7 (2)	19 (4)	
p. Mother separated from child since release or first interview			
No	52%(14)	100%(21)	$p < .001$
Yes	26 (7)	—	
Does not apply, not reunited	22 (6)	—	
q. Mother's report whether child worries she will go away again			
Yes	32%(8)		
No	52 (13)		
Mother does not know	12 (3)		
Does not apply	4 (1)		

Chi-square (χ^2) tests of statistical significance are used in all tables. N.S. indicates that χ^2 was not significant at the .05 level.

father who fled with the child and was untraceable, and children who remained in foster care. In most of these cases, the mothers wanted to regain custody of their children. In at least one case the mother had done nothing to facilitate her children's return, and it appeared unlikely that she would take any immediate action.

The mothers who had been reunited with their children were asked how soon after their release they had seen their children. The majority had seen them on the day of release, but others several days later.

Only one-third of the released mothers were living in the same residence they occupied prior to their incarceration (table 13-3e). The mothers who returned to the same residence were usually those who lived with their parents. The residential change experienced by the majority of the jail mothers was significantly different from probation mothers, approximately three-quarters of whom were living in the same residence as at the time they began probation.

After release, 30 percent of the jail mothers had not resumed living with their children, 22 percent were living with their children alone, 22 percent with their children and their own parents, 11 percent with their children and husband or male companion, and 15 percent with their children and others. All probation mothers were living with their children at time II, most with the children alone and others with an adult male or the child's grandparents (table 13-3f).

Mothers were asked whether their children inquired about their sentences. There was a significant difference between the two groups: 55 percent of the jail children asked their mothers about jail whereas only 26 percent of the probation children asked about probation (table 13-3c). The different level of questioning at time II is understandable in light of the fact that, according to the mothers, 89 percent of the jail and only 53 percent of the probation children knew about the sentences (table 13-3b).

In response to their children's questions about jail, mothers described their experience as either negative or tolerable, but never positive (table 13-3g). In dealing with young children, mothers tended to downplay the experience and minimize the situation. Mothers typically said they missed the child while they were gone and that it was not a place the child would want to go. They said that children aged 9 to 13 were more curious about the jail and sometimes were teasing in their inquiries. Mothers of preadolescents frequently mentioned that they used their own experience of being punished in jail to lecture their child about the hazards of breaking the law. Jail was sometimes used as a threat to children of this age for misbehavior. Mothers of teenagers occasionally made moralistic comments about their jail experience, but more often gave realistic accounts of what happened in jail. The mother would talk about her acquaintances in jail and various staff members. Some mothers reported they felt awkward discussing their jail experiences with their children and hoped that it would be forgotten as soon as possible. A minority of the mothers mentioned that the topic came up with regularity because they were currently seeing women they had met in jail on a social basis, which prompted comments about jail.

During the first interview at time I it was clear to the interviewers that some children were visibly upset and others tense when discussing their mother's absence. Occasionally the interviewers had to interrupt the sessions to allow the children to regain composure. At the second interview, after being reunited with their mothers, the separation had become a less immediate and sensitive issue. The children's willingness to discuss their mothers' incarceration with their acquaintances also increased. More jail children discussed the mother's criminal status at time II (17 percent) than at time I (3 percent). There was somewhat less lying and evading the issue after the mother was home (table 13-3*d*).

Not all the children acknowledged the mother's incarceration as a matter of choice. Helen G., a high school sophomore whose mother was convicted of embezzlement, reported that while her mother was in jail she had told only her best friend about it and had sworn her friend to secrecy. At time II, she felt uneasy that other people at school knew about her mother and were talking about her behind her back. When asked how she handled this situation, Helen said she would briefly acknowledge her mother's conviction, but she never raised the subject. She also said she tried to place herself above the situation by disassociating herself from her mother's activities. Helen considered her mother's conviction a social burden and she resented it.

In another family, Audrey W., an overweight 13-year-old daughter of a mother convicted of forgery, ran away two weeks after her mother returned home from jail. The mother's comment about her daughter was, "It's strange she runs away now—now that things are back to normal." When the mother was asked if she felt there might be any connection between her daughter's running away and her own conviction and sentence, she said there might be, though it did not make any sense.

Asked whether their children told other people about their incarceration and how they felt about it, 44 percent of the mothers said their children did not tell other people, 15 percent said they did not know, and 11 percent said their children did not know. The remaining mothers whose children told other people about the incarceration said they did not mind (18 percent) or they disliked it (11 percent). The 18 percent who did not mind their children telling others shrugged it off as the truth, so why complain. Those who disliked it said it made them unhappy (table 13-3*h*).

In general, the children's reactions seemed more intense while the mother was in jail. Her incarceration had a direct bearing on them and her absence was of immediate concern to them. After the mother's release, though her conviction was of less immediate concern and less an impingement upon the children, it was not a forgotten matter.

Mothers were asked whether their children behaved any differently toward them since their release from jail. According to 59 percent of the mothers, their children acted just the same toward them as they had prior to the jail term. While none of the mothers reported that their children's attitude toward them had improved, 30 percent said their children's behavior toward them had worsened (table 13-3*i*). Typical reports of worse behavior were that the child showed less respect, talked back more often, and used more profanity.

Raoul H., a 16-year-old son of a Mexican-born mother who had been convicted of using stolen credit cards, avoided discussing things with his mother with whom he had formerly had a close relationship. He said he was no longer able to confide in her because she could not be trusted. Raoul and the rest of the family had been totally unaware of the mother's illegal activities, and he remained unsympathetic to her explanations.

In most cases the mothers did not give much thought to the questions about the children's attitudes toward them and answered offhandedly. The responses seemed to reflect superficial consideration on their part rather than deliberate evasion of the subject.

Asked about their children's general behavior, both in and out of the home, since their release, 44 percent of the mothers reported no changes in the children's behavior, 26 percent worse behavior, and 11 percent improved behavior (table 13-3*j*). The reports of worse behavior primarily involved disciplinary problems. The majority of the mothers were relieved that after a period of adjustment things were returning to normal; their children had their own activities and were mentioning the mother's absence with less frequency.

Mothers were asked whether their children had been in trouble recently with the police, at school, or with the neighbors. There was no significant difference between the jail and the probation children, since most had not been in any serious trouble (table 13-3*k*).

In terms of their own adjustment, mothers were asked about their current employment status. Most of the jail mothers, 89 percent, were not employed. Of those unemployed, 38 percent were looking for a job while the other 62 percent were not (table 13-3*l*). The few mothers who were employed usually had different jobs from those held prior to their arrest. It was not surprising that most of the jail mothers who sought work were still unemployed so shortly after their release. If a woman had a job at the time of her arrest, she usually lost it when she went to jail. While serving time, there was little opportunity to seek employment. Although the jails had rehabilitation workers to help the inmates find gainful employment on release, in fact only one jail in this study, Santa Clara, made any noticeable effort to assist women in finding jobs. Santa Clara also had a work furlough program through which some inmates were released during the day and were able to get job training or work in the community while they served their sentences.

Mothers were asked, at time II, what their greatest problem had been recently. There was a significant difference between the responses given by the jail and probation mothers. Over half of the probation mothers reported they had no new problems. The jail mothers most frequently mentioned financial difficulties and finding a job as problems (41 percent). Getting settled again was the second most frequently mentioned problem (37 percent). Only 11 percent of the jail mothers reported they had no new problems after release (table 13-3o). During the initial jail interview, mothers were asked to anticipate their problems on release: 19 percent expected financial problems (table 13-3n). This was apparently an underestimation of the problem. In addition to other financial concerns, mothers frequently had difficulty finding affordable housing and getting settled again.

By the time of the second interview, approximately one month after the mother's release from jail, a striking 26 percent of the jail mothers, that is one-third of those who were reunited with their children, reported they had been separated again from their children for at least a few days and sometimes longer (table 13-3p). In one case, a mother who was interviewed was in jail again on a new offense. At least two of the "lost" mothers were incarcerated again outside the counties included in this study. Personal reasons such as illness and lack of finances were typically given for the recent separations from the children. One mother took a trip to southern California to visit a boyfriend in prison. Other mothers mentioned day trips or occasional nights away from home, but these were not considered separations for the purposes of this study.

The frequent separation suggests that many of these mothers were unwilling or unable to successfully adjust to the responsibilities of caring for their children again and resuming their personal lives after release. Some mothers displayed indifference to the possibility that their children might be unsettled by another separation. None of the probation mothers, however, reported any separations from their children during the time period between the first and second interviews.

Perhaps the most deeply felt result of this recurrent pattern of separation was that many of the jail children expressed a strong fear that their mothers would leave them again. Thirty percent of the jail mothers reported they noticed some anxiety in their children about their leaving again (table 13-3q). Mothers reported being asked especially by younger children whether she was going away again. They tried to reassure their children, but expressed uncertainty at how successful they had been.

One mother, who had cooperated with the prosecutor and supplied information about local drug traffic, recalled that on the day of her release, her 12-year-old son called her into the living room and in a self-conscious manner asked her please not to have anything more to do with drugs. It was too dangerous, he argued, and it hurt everyone in the family. The mother was greatly impressed with him and told this anecdote with apparent pride.

The findings in this study support the hypothesis that most jail children are reunited with their mothers after her release. Further evidence obtained at the follow-up interviews suggests that this period after reunion involves some instability and is characterized by problems for the mothers and often some anxiety for the children. The reunited mothers and children could not be considered stable family units.

Discussion

The impact of incarceration does not end with the release of the mother from jail. The return of the mother into the community and to her family creates problems of readjustment for mother and child, both individually and in their relationship to each other.

The mother's problems upon release are more outwardly apparent than those of her children. Even a woman who leaves jail with a strong determination to avoid future criminal involvement and to strengthen her family's unity will encounter difficult and discouraging prospects. One of the first problems a woman is likely to encounter is that of financially supporting her family. Two-fifths of the women in this study mentioned acute financial problems upon release. Those who intended to reestablish their status on welfare complained of the red tape and possible delays before receipt of payments. In one case a woman reported having to borrow money from a local loan shark to meet expenses until welfare support resumed. Other women found themselves dependent upon the generosity of relatives and friends.

Women who sought employment after release reported little success. Three-fourths of the mothers who sought work had been unsuccessful during the first month. One woman felt she must find employment and an apartment of her own before she could regain and support her children who were then living in a foster home. The only job she could find was working nights in a pharmacy. After a month's time a former boyfriend reappeared causing her to lose her job and to postpone again her efforts to regain custody of her children.

Finding a suitable place to live was an immediate problem for many of the women upon release. Most of these women looked for and found residences in the same area where they had lived prior to incarceration. This helped minimize problems of relocation, but returned them to a similar social environment to the one in which they had lived before their arrest.

Social life was mainly confined to old friends, relatives, and former acquaintances. One mother had been divorced while she was in jail and several others had been deserted by boyfriends. The lack of a stable intimate relationship was one of the main causes of stress for many.

A woman released from jail faces numerous pressures associated with reestablishing her life outside. These problems—financial, occupational, residential, and social—cannot help but create stressful pressures at a time when a mother is trying to reestablish an interrupted relationship with her children. How she copes with these stresses will have an important impact on her children and on her relationship with them. Other studies of women under stress have shown that during the first year following a divorce, households of divorced mothers with children were always more disorganized than those of intact families (Hetherington et al, 1975, 1976). Children of jail mothers, like children of divorced mothers, must contend with mothers who are undergoing a period of relative stress. These children cannot fully understand adult pressures but, generally, do not feel comfortable with what is happening and may even feel threatened. Children commonly resist change and their behavior may become more disobedient and resistant to parental authority at a time when the mother may be making unprecedented demands of them. The fact that jailed as well as divorced mothers often experience a breakdown in communications with children and find they have less control over their behavior suggests that these are common results of failure to cope with pressures, distinct from the specific circumstances of such events as release from jail or divorce.

The child's problems upon the release of the mother from jail are often less apparent but may have just as penetrating and long-term effects. Children were often forced to cope with changes in residence, possibly a change in school, as well as a readjustment to a mother who has serious problems of her own and occasionally a new living companion. Children repeatedly expressed fear of future separation and exhibited some behavioral problems, including less obedience to their mother. Some children said they were now less trusting of their mothers than they had been before. A few said they thought of their mother differently after she was out of jail, but had trouble articulating exactly how they felt.

Children are usually unable to comprehend the stress that their mother feels from outside sources. To them, financial problems mean the mother has less money to spend on them. Employment reduces the amount of time the mother has to spend with them. Moving may mean having to leave old friends and necessitate meeting new people. It would be unrealistic not to expect a child's problems to affect his attitudes and behavior, and consequently his relationship with his mother might suffer. Children react to stress in less predictable ways than their mothers. Children have to draw on their own resources to find ways of dealing with disturbing situations which they are seldom prepared for. It is not surprising then to find their reactions ranging from avoidance to desperation to the absurd. In this study, shortly after the mother's release, one girl ran away from home, one young boy refused to speak to his mother for several days, an older boy lectured his mother on the dangers of drug use, and another girl expressed disappointment when her mother did not bring her a present from jail. Perhaps the girl's request for a gift was an attempt on her part to equate the mother's time in jail with her previous absences from home. In this manner, perhaps the girl sought the mother's complicity in the child's refusal to acknowledge the mother's incarceration.

Some children who visited their mother frequently while she was in jail displayed a more complacent acceptance of the mother upon her release. Their exposure to the mother in jail allowed them opportunities to assimilate their mother's situation and helped ease the confrontation upon release.

How both the mother and the child deal with their problems affects the future cohesion of the family. The immediate attention given by some mothers to their personal problems caused either a delay in reunion or periods of subsequent separation. These concerns detracted from the attention they could give their children. It is understandable that some women felt the need to cope with their own urgent problems of employment, housing, and personal readjustment before the less obvious needs of their children. Only a few showed much success in coping with both at the same time. One mother who wanted to see her boyfriend, a fieldworker in central California, took her child out of school for several days to accompany her. She explained she felt it was more important they not be separated again so soon than that the child miss a few more days of school. This mother showed some insight to her child's needs as well as her own and was one of the mothers who reported few behavioral problems. There seems to be lack of awareness on the part of these mothers, rather than a deliberate disregard of the consequences their actions may have on the children. In only a minority of cases did a mother's self-interest seem so predominant that she willfully ignored the welfare of her child.

This study found that in all cases the mother's incarceration caused a disruption in the children's lives and in many cases resulted in a less stable family unit after her release. The most serious erosion of family ties was found in families in which the incarceration was merely one in a series of disruptions.

All too often the community at large feels well served when criminal activity results in imprisonment. Seldom does the community consider what effect jail terms may have on offenders and their dependents. Under the present penal system, little is done inside jails to bring about rehabilitation or to deter future criminal activity. Consideration must be given to the relative social merit of incarceration when weighed against the serious implications this punishment may have on the children inadvertently involved. Serious consideration should be given to allowing parents to retain custody of their children while serving a sentence and to the development of other means of social control.

14 Final Discussion

In recent years there have been increasing numbers of women arrested for criminal offenses. Female arrests for serious crimes were up 2.9 percent in 1978 and according to the lastest FBI Uniform Crime Report, 19.9 percent of the arrests for Crime Index Offenses were of females (U.S. Department of Justice, 1979). As more women become involved in the criminal justice system, it is important that the social costs of various types of criminal sanctions are appreciated. The predicament of convicted mothers and their children is especially complex and demands attention.

This study was designed as an exploratory investigation of children separated from their incarcerated mothers. Information was gathered in four counties about incarcerated mothers and their children. In the following sections summary observations are made about the findings of this study, programs available for offenders with children elsewhere are described, and recommendations are made for further research as well as for jail reforms.

With so many women in jails and prisons many individual differences are found, and there is no pattern to which all mothers and children conform. Therefore, caution is exercised in drawing any final conclusions and in making any generalizations based on this study which is necessarily tied to a particular time and place. It is hoped, however, that knowledge gained concerning the circumstances of incarceration will contribute to the understanding of the effects of maternal separation.

Summary

Who are these mothers that are going to jail? In the present study they were young, poorly educated women, often of an ethnic minority. Typically, they had children at a very young age and had unstable marital relationships, if indeed they had any ongoing relationships. Consequently, many of these women were living alone with their children. The women were from the lowest socioeconomic levels and most were unemployed and dependent upon welfare for support. Drug use, addiction, and to a lesser extent alcoholism were common among them. More than half had friends who had been incarcerated, and more than half had parents or siblings who also had been in jail or prison.

Why are these mothers being sent to jail? All the jailed women in this study pled guilty to criminal charges, and the court determined that they should serve a sentence in jail rather than be placed on probation. Most were convicted of property offenses. This conforms to national statistics which show females arrested most commonly for larceny-theft offenses (U.S. Department of Justice, 1979). Others were convicted for either narcotic offenses or violent crimes. Although less than half of the jailed mothers had juvenile records, over half had prior adult arrests, half had been on probation previously, and almost half had a prior incarceration. A woman's employment at the time of arrest was more important than the particular offense or her criminal background in determining whether she would be sentenced to jail by the court.

The women's children in this study were almost all of school age (4 to 18 years old) and all had been living with their mother at the time of arrest. Many of these women also had children of preschool age who were not included in this study.

The children experienced multiple disruptions in their lives. In the mother's absence they were cared for by others, usually grandparents, fathers, or other relatives. Over one-third of the children had more than one living arrangement during the mother's incarceration, typically the consequence of a hurried placement of a child with a friend or neighbor. Most siblings remained together, but one-fourth of the children were separated from brothers or sisters. Generally the caretakers did not treat the temporary custody of the children as a burden and most received welfare funds for the children's care.

Although it is common and highly acceptable for mothers in jail to express concern about their children, jail mothers were actually very poorly informed when asked factual questions about their children. Most mothers were able to give the grade level of their child, but were less able to give the name of the school, the name of the teacher, or the names of their child's friends. It can be assumed that this lack of knowledge will increase during the mother's period of incarceration. It was interesting to note that the children were either more reluctant than mothers to reveal the mother's lack of information about their friends and school activities or they were simply unaware of it.

Almost all the jail children were aware of their mother's incarceration, even though some of the mothers had tried, for a time, to conceal this information. Many had been present at the time of their mother's arrest, and still others had accompanied her to a court session. However, even though approximately two-thirds of the children visited their mothers in jail at least once, they frequently had vague, often inaccurate, notions of the conditions inside a jail and were uncertain when their mother would be released. It was evident that most of the children considered it inappropriate to discuss their mother's circumstances with outsiders.

During incarceration, some mothers in all four jails in this study received visits from their children, regardless of age. The visiting facilities and policies of each jail played significant roles in determining whether the mother and child found their visits satisfactory and whether the mother encouraged the child to visit again. Jails that permitted physical contact between mother and child under nonoppressive conditions and allowed private conversation were the most desirable. Facilities that tended to discourage visits had glass or screen barriers in cramped and crowded quarters. Satisfactory visits appeared to lower a child's anxiety about his mother's absence and provided a link between the mother and her family. Contact by telephone was sporadic and difficult and contact through letters was rare. Neither appeared to be an adequate substitute for personal visits.

Children of incarcerated mothers had considerable exposure to the criminal justice system. In addition to the exposure a child had through his mother, most had seen other people arrested and a few of the older children had been in trouble with the police themselves. The children reported a willingness to seek the assistance of the police when they needed help but older children had some reluctance to report the criminal activity of others to the police. Approximately half of the jail children expressed interest in becoming police officers, though this was less true of the older children. In no case did a child who had witnessed the arrest of the mother when force was used want to become a police officer. Likewise, children of jail mothers who had attended a court session with their mothers were unlikely to want to become police officers and usually had a negative impression of the police. It appears that children who had contacts with the police and courts which resulted in negative consequences for the mother generally had negative feelings about the police.

The questions intended to ascertain the children's legal reasoning met with general failure because they were unable to answer many of them. Due to the low-response rate, it was not possible to satisfactorily assess the children's legal reasoning by the method used.

Children of offenders did poorly in school. Long-term factors of low-socioeconomic status and the mother's criminal record were more influential than her current incarceration in causing the children's poor performance. Also many of these children had changed schools several times. There appeared to be a widespread incidence of behavioral problems and low self-esteem among jail children as reported by their teachers. Given the importance the community puts on education, prolonged poor academic performance appears to be a discouraging sign.

The welfare status of the children of incarcerated mothers remained unchanged. Most of the children had been supported by Aid to Families with Dependent Children (AFDC) before the mother's arrest and most continued to be dependent upon welfare during her sentence and after her release. The unemployed mothers complained that employment opportunities became even scarcer after they had a criminal record.

Most of the mothers and children were reunited after the mother's release from jail. The high incidence of subsequent separations within the first month, along with the likelihood of recidivism, suggests that future disruptions in the mother-child relationship can be expected in many instances. Interruptions in the mother's child-caring role had become an established pattern for some. Mothers often reported their children had become less respectful and were harder to control since their release. These domestic problems were compounded by the mother's financial and housing relocation difficulties, as well as her personal readjustment.

One of the most provocative findings of this study was that nowhere in the course of the legal process were the children of arrested women considered as participants in the proceedings. At the time of arrest, police officers do not necessarily inquire if there are children. If the mother is detained, the care of the children falls on the family, relatives, neighbors, or the children themselves. At the time of the court proceedings the existence of children is not necessarily mentioned either. Even if the court chose to consider the children, no procedure exists for the court to utilize. If the children are considered at all, it is in the presentence report filed by the probation department. After a woman has pled guilty or been found guilty at trial, the probation office is usually requested to conduct a background report and, on that basis, to recommend a sentence, either probation or incarceration. No further action is taken by the probation department if the mother is sentenced to jail. The court assumes no responsibility for the child's placement during the mother's incarceration. It is possible that if the courts were made aware of the children and their involvement in the mother's situation, and if channels for proceeding existed, perhaps when the courts imposed sentence they might choose to recognize responsibility for the children.

Also when the woman is serving her sentence, the jail staff is typically unaware of the existence and whereabouts of an inmate's children. No records are made of this seemingly relevant information. Likewise, few attempts are made to facilitate the mother-child relationship. There are no specific visitation periods designed for children, no staff consultants available to deal with family problems, and no attempt made to shelter children from vicariously sharing this negative jail experience. In fact, this study found that the jails did not recognize any responsibility or show any interest in the children of inmates.

The period of incarceration does bring about a serious division in the mother-child relationship. And though most of the women and children are reunited, there is evidence that this separation could have enduring effects. It is generally believed that it is in society's best interests to maintain family units, especially for young children. Since jail mothers are often single parental figures, the erosion of this important family tie is bound to have deleterious consequences for the child, perhaps for the mother and society. Recognizing this, in severe cases the community must be prepared to take the responsibility for removing these children from their mothers and providing for suitable upbringing.

While women are in jail, little is done to alleviate the social and economic conditions which may have contributed to their criminal behavior. Consequently, there is reason for believing these women will resume their previous activities upon release. This suggests an ongoing pattern of discontinuous parental supervision for the children. In other words, while incarceration seems to have served the letter of the law, it has done nothing to prevent recidivism and nothing to improve a child's chances for a normal upbringing. While the community may feel itself well served by the process of imprisonment, little consideration is given to the children, who are themselves members of society and feel the immediate effects.

Another interesting finding of this study was that the impact of a mother's incarceration did not, in and of itself, determine a child's attitude toward the police, in particular, and the laws of the community, in general. This means that most of these children remain susceptible to positive community standards. Legal attitudes are considered to be evolving concepts. What this suggests is that there are opportunities for the community to counterbalance any negative experiences with some positive measures.

Upon their release, most of the mothers attempted to reunify their families, but because of their limited awareness, did very little to constructively deal with whatever problems their incarceration may have caused their children. Interviews with these women after their release suggest that they would willingly and conscientiously do much more to alleviate their children's anxieties. Therefore any counseling or advice that could be made available to mothers before or upon release might be very beneficial in readjustment with their children.

In summary, while some recent public attention has focused on the female offender—her motives and her crimes—very little attention has been given to the plight of the children of these women. A great deal remains to be done in thoroughly examining this situation and in developing new ways to deal with convicted parents.

Programs for Offenders with Children

Innovative programs are needed to recognize the familial ties and responsibilities of offenders and preserve the family unit when a parent is sentenced. Although few special programs affecting families are available in local county jails, several approaches have been developed in state and federal correctional institutions. The goals of the various projects include efforts to facilitate visits, ease the separation adjustments, provide the mother opportunities to improve parenting skills, and keep the parent and child together. No program can establish a stable loving relationship between an incarcerated parent and child but a program can help maintain family ties.

Several surveys of correctional institutions describe programs including parent education, special visiting schedules for children, and home furloughs (American Bar Association, 1976; Contact, Inc., 1978; McGowan & Blumenthal, 1978; Musk, 1979). Most state institutions have only general visiting schedules that permit visits ranging from one hour twice a month to daily visits not exceeding an hour. About a dozen states have special visiting schedules for children allowing all-day visits or weekend stays, with restrictions based on the mother's status in the institution and the child's age. For example, the Iowa Women's Reformatory has a visitation project designed for preschoolers scheduled monthly. The Bedford Hills Correctional Facility in New York has a Sesame Street Program that provides activities for children during the regular weekend visiting hours. Besides providing recreation for the children, one of the objects of this program is to provide time for adults to visit alone. The New Jersey Correctional Institute for Women has a federally funded program that attempts to ensure at least one visit per month for inmate mothers and includes a weekend camp retreat with activities for mothers and children.

The Purdy Treatment Center for Women in Washington emphasizes the importance of the family in the correctional process. Inmates' children are placed in foster homes close to the prison and inmate mothers participate in the selection of the homes. Children are encouraged to visit in the women's living quarters and mothers are permitted to visit in the foster homes. A nursery school is operated at Purdy four days a week for children from the neighboring community and once a week for children of inmates.

Education for mothers is emphasized in child development classes for women in the Maryland Correctional Institution for Women and the Ohio Reformatory for Women. The Nebraska Center for Women and the Arizona State Prison have Mother-Offspring Life Development (MOLD) programs that include children's overnight visits at the institution, nursery programs, child-care classes, counseling, and evaluation. The Minnesota Correctional Institution for Women has a federally funded program called Second Chance that includes weekend visits for children, weekly seminars, discussion groups, counseling, assistance with family matters, and child-care training in a community Head Start program which is located at the institution.

Institutions in a few states allow infants to stay in the institution with the mothers. Ohio and North Carolina have newborns in their institution hospitals for short periods until outside care arrangements can be made. Infants born during incarceration are allowed to stay up to one year in New York and up to eighteen months in Florida.

California has long had legislation allowing young children to remain with their imprisoned mothers, though it has not been implemented. In a 1976 case, a California superior court held that a prison superintendent may use reasonable discretion to deny an incarcerated mother the right to keep her child with her in prison (*Cardell* v. *Enomoto*, No. 701-094, 1976). After that decision, new legislation was passed and took effect in 1979 which requires the Department of Corrections to establish and implement a community treatment program by 1980 for women who have children under age 2 years and 2 months (Appendix K). This pilot program was based on a legislative finding that the separation of infants from their mothers, while the mothers are in prison, can cause serious psychological damage to infants. The new legislation is intended to alleviate the harm to infants by providing for the release of the mother and child to public or private facilities in the community. The Department of Corrections is directed to establish a safe and wholesome environment for the participating children, using the least restrictive alternative to incarceration and restraint possible to achieve the objectives of correction and consistent with public safety and justice.

The eligibility requirements specify that the California program is limited to women who have two years or less to serve, who have not previously served time in a state prison, who were the primary caretakers of their children, whose children are 2 years and 2 months old or less, who have not been found to be unfit parents, and who have applied to the program within thirty days of custody. When a woman applies for the program, she may be subject to a fitness proceeding and if she has been convicted of a violent crime or addicted to any drug, there is a presumption in favor of challenging her fitness as a parent.

The criteria have been criticized for being so restrictive that only a very small number of presently imprisoned women would be eligible for the program (Barry, 1979). There are also limitations to the statute's implementation, inconsistencies in its language, and possible constitutional problems. Because of these shortcomings and its novelty, the operation of the California program should be carefully evaluated before it is rejected or adopted as a model for reform.

Another prototype project, the Women's Residential Center, has recently begun in Santa Clara County in California (Black, 1979). This is an alternative to county jail in which inmate mothers and their children are housed in apartments. The mothers work or receive job training during the day while the children attend school or day care. It is a very promising effort to permit mothers and children to remain together in a community setting while the mother serves her sentence. The program stresses responsibility and offers guidance and assistance in employment, household management, and child care.

Only a few small projects around the country, including one that began operation in San Francisco in 1979, provide legal services specifically for incarcerated parents (Barry, 1979). Incarcerated parents have need of legal assistance in matters involving their children (Botler, 1979). There are a number of prisoners' legal services offices throughout the country and even a few organizations which focus on the legal needs of incarcerated women. These projects are typically supported by foundation and grant money and occasionally are associated with a law school clinic. Limited resources and time require most prisoners' legal assistance agencies to limit the number of clients and types of cases they handle. It would be desirable to have legal assistance more widely available to all inmates.

Model Sentencing and Corrections Act

The National Conference of Commissioners on Uniform State Laws has recommended a model sentencing and corrections act containing provisions dealing with incarcerated parents and their children for consideration by all states (Appendix L). This is a semiofficial organization sponsored by the states to propose legislation in areas where uniformity of law is appropriate. The model act could be an important development if states are prompted to revise their statutes along the proposed lines. The objectives of the drafters were to establish a fair system of sentencing criminal offenders, organize a state correctional agency, authorize correctional programs, and define the legal rights of confined persons.

The drafters of the model act concluded that conviction and incarceration should not deprive a person of parental rights or justify state action affecting parents and children. The act rejects the notion that disruption of the parental relationship by confinement is part of the penalty imposed for a crime. Nor does it endorse leniency in sentencing an offender solely because the offender has a child. Instead it recommends that the state assume an affirmative obligation to assist incarcerated persons to meet their parental responsibilities and permit housing children with their parents in correctional settings. The model act would apply to confined mothers and fathers and without age limit for the children. The act provides that the director of corrections must assist incarcerated persons in communicating with their children and otherwise keeping informed of their affairs, and participating in decisions relating to the custody, care, and instruction of their children.

The model act would permit incarcerated parents to retain physical custody of a child during incarceration under the discretion of the director, with certain conditions. If the parent requested the child reside in the facility, the director would be required to consider (1) the best interests of the child and the confined person, (2) the length of sentence and the likelihood that the child could remain throughout the term, (3) the suitability of the facilities, (4) available alternatives that would protect and strengthen the parent-child relationship, and (5) the age of the child.

There are also provisions in the model act to protect the interests of the child so that a child may not reside in a facility if (1) the parent has been certified physically or emotionally unable to care for the child, (2) the condition of the facility will result in a substantial detriment to the physical or emotional well-being of the child, or (3) a court orders that the child not reside in the facility.

Professor Harvey Perlman has suggested that instead of viewing the issue as whether there should be programs implemented at the discretion of correctional administrators, the more fundamental legal issue is the extent of permissible state intrusion into family relationships (Perlman, 1979). He asserts that confined parents retain their rights to preserve parental relationships and to continue to exercise parental responsibilities, including physical custody of children. This should include wide but not unlimited discretion on the part of inmate parents to decide whether to keep a child with them in an institution or place the child elsewhere.

If attempts to preserve parental relationships are viewed as programs designed to benefit parents or children rather than as basic rights, such reforms may not be broadly implemented. A perspective based on parental rights undermines arguments that present jail and prison conditions preclude housing children with parents. Although the current conditions of most institutions are unsuitable for children, it should be possible to develop correctional facilities and programs that could accommodate prisoners' families.

Further Research

Innovations in the treatment of convicted parents will be of only limited value unless they are carefully evaluated for their impact on families. Studies of programs that keep parents and children together while the parent serves a sentence will be important because these projects could become prototypes of alternatives to the standard practice of incarceration.

Further research is being done on the effects of separation caused by parental incarceration (Baunach, 1979; Owens, 1979; Savage, 1979), including a study about the psychological effects on school-aged children caused by maternal imprisonment (LaPoint & Radke-Yarrow, 1979).

To more thoroughly examine the effects of having a parent incarcerated, longitudinal studies should be conducted in which children and inmate parents are studied at various stages throughout their lives so that any long-term trends in their assimilation of this experience could be observed. Selected in-depth studies would be a means of enriching a longitudinal study.

Children under 4 years old should be included in any further study of offenders' children. Many of the parents in jail and prison are young adults with infants and preschool-age children. The special separation problems of young children deserve attention, and these early experiences may be important in later development.

The effect of a father's incarceration on children deserves thorough investigation. Supplemental studies concerning the effects of incarceration on spouses and on adult relationships as well as the effects of the incarceration of siblings should be considered.

Useful policy recommendations for child-custody arrangements when a parent is incarcerated should be based on knowledge of what happens to families under these circumstances.

Recommendations

There is no simple solution to the problems that confront children of incarcerated parents. Fundamental issues concerning the conflicting interests of children, parents, and the state need to be addressed. Under most circumstances it is preferable to preserve family relationships and to allow parents who have the responsibility for the custody and care of children to make decisions concerning them. At the same time, the parens patriae tradition reflects a notion that the state has a special responsibility to protect children, even from their parents. Before coherent policies and programs for children and families are possible, the objectives of the criminal justice and child welfare systems also require clarification.

Conviction and criminal punishment should not destroy family relationships. Greater recognition of the parental rights and responsibilities of convicted persons will require reconsideration of the present use of incarceration as the primary means of punishment. If the state deprives a child of parental care because of incarceration, it should assume an obligation to assist inmates in maintaining family ties, meeting their parental responsibilities, and minimizing harm to the child.

Based on the findings of this study, some recommendations can be made to improve the present situation of families separated because of parental incarceration. At the time of arrest, efforts should be made to minimize the potential harm and trauma to the children when they are present. Arresting officers should always inquire whether an adult is responsible for any dependents. Some opportunity should be available so that a parent can make arrangements for the child's care and explain the situation to the child. If the parent is unable to make arrangements, a referral should be made to a child welfare agency.

Pretrial investigations should include a report of the defendant's family responsibilities. Guidelines should be developed for detention procedures in cases of persons with dependents. Information about placement alternatives for children should be available to parents at the time of pretrial detention and sentencing. It would also be useful to develop clear guidelines regarding the status of parental rights upon conviction and the grounds for terminating parental rights in appropriate cases. A legal rights handbook for parents that could be distributed to all inmates with dependent children would be valuable to inform them about the law and their rights and responsibilities.

At the present time when a woman enters jail, no record is made of whether she has any dependents. Gathering of this information should be a first step in dealing with domestic problems. Further steps might logically follow. For example, a staff member or volunteer could contact these mothers after their arrival and act as a liaison to their families if necessary. Some volunteer organizations along these lines have developed, particularly in men's facilities, that could serve as models for women's institutions. Regular group sessions for mothers of young children who were interested in learning about child care and sharing their problems and concerns could be established. Counseling should be available to deal with the problems of adjustment during the separation and in anticipation of the difficulties of readjustment upon release. Legal assistance should be available to resolve any legal problems.

Special attention should be given to establishing better visitation conditions for young children. At present, most visiting facilities and regulations are designed solely for adult visitors. This study found that without some physical contact and some opportunity for intimacy, visits with children were generally unsatisfactory. Jails should establish visiting periods and facilities that are more conducive to relaxed visits than the usual high-security visiting area. Longer visiting periods would also be desirable when young children are involved.

Standardizing the regulations for telephone use and providing reasonable access for calls to families would do much to facilitate continuing communication between parents and children. Irregular and limited phone access prevents a mother from establishing a routine of talking to her child and makes it difficult to deal with ongoing or emergency family matters. At present, children are unable to contact their mothers by phone at any time. It would be a considerable improvement if jails established simple, understandable policies that would permit incoming calls from members of the immediate family. Evidence indicates that mothers and children do not frequently supplement limited visits and phone calls with writing letters. Although it would be unrealistic to expect much correspondence, stationery and postage should be available.

More could be done in jail to provide useful job training and opportunities for finding employment after release. Much more programming is done in prisons than in jails in this regard. Work furlough and home furlough programs should be organized. Assistance in finding employment and housing could help alleviate some of the most serious difficulties inmates encounter upon release.

Improving conditions for parents in jail is sometimes easier to implement than expected. A graphic example of this occurred as the present study was concluding. Upon observing the differences in visiting conditions among the four jails studied, attention was drawn to what appeared to be unnecessarily severe and oppressive visiting conditions in San Francisco's San Bruno jail. Initially, when this was brought to the attention of the jail director, all suggestions for improvement met with unyielding opposition. However, when these conditions were brought to the attention of the sheriff's office, a meeting was arranged with the undersheriff who had responsibility for the jail and the director to discuss children's visitation. Upon examination, it was discovered that changes in visitation policy could be made without compromising security or overtaxing the staff. Within a month's time, with the help of volunteers, a revised visiting policy permitting contact visits took effect on a trial basis. This innovation was welcomed by the inmates and was soon adopted as the standard visitation policy. Desirable reforms that are practical can be pursued with some hope of success.

The problem of the female offender in contemporary society has established itself in the public consciousness. It is hoped that in the near future a similar public awareness and concern will extend to the children of offenders. Innovation and research will increase our knowledge and ability to deal with family relationships more successfully.

Appendix A
Interview Forms

Mothers' Interview
Time I

Questions marked * to be asked *only* of jail mothers.
Questions marked ** to be asked *only* of probation mothers.
Questions not marked to be asked of both jail and probation mothers.

1. Children's names   Sex   Age

    _____   _____   _____

    _____   _____   _____

    _____   _____   _____

    _____   _____   _____

    _____   _____   _____

2. Just before you were arrested, or got involved with the law, who did your children live with?
   If mother lived with child
     Where?
     How long did you live there?
   If *child* was living with someone else
     Why was he staying there?
     How long had he been staying there?

3. Have there been any changes in where your child has been staying since that time? (yes/no)
   If yes: What was the change?
           Why was there a change?

4. Who else lives with *child*?

5. Did *child* stay in the same school or did he change schools?
   What school does he go to now?
   What grade is he in?
   What is his teacher's name?

6. Who has legal custody of your child?

7. How was *child* being supported before you were arrested?
   How is he being supported now?

8. Were you arrested? (yes/no)
   If yes: When?
          Where?
          What were you arrested for?
   If no: How did you get involved with the law?

9. Were you detained or held in custody by the police at the time of your arrest? (or when you got involved with the law or when you turned yourself in?) (yes/no)

If yes: How long?
 Were you able to make any phone calls after you were arrested?
 Who did you call?
 Did you make arrangements for the care of your child at that time or did
   someone else take care of that? (yes/no) If someone else, who?
 Who did your child stay with right after you were arrested?
 Did _____ come to stay with *child* or did *child* go to stay
   with _____?

10. Was *child* present when you were arrested this time or any other time? This time?
    Earlier time? (yes/no)
    If yes: (If *child* present at several arrests, describe each separate episode.)
       Please describe what happened. Where? When? Handcuffs?
       Did the police talk to *child*?
       How did the police act toward *child*? (polite, gruff, kind, ignored him?)
       How did *child* act during arrest? (frightened, crying, puzzled, calm?)
       How did *child* act afterward?
       Did *child* understand what happened? (yes/no)
    If no: (*Child* was not present this time.)
       Was he told about the arrest? (yes/no)
       If yes: What was he told?
            Who told him?
            How did *child* act when he was told that?
       If no: Why did you decide not to tell him?

11. Have the police ever been to your house when *child* was home at any time?
    (yes/no)
    If yes: What were the circumstances? (to help in an emergency, to question you
        about something, to search the house, earlier arrest, called by you,
        other?)

12. Do you know how *child* feels about policemen? (frightened, trusting, etc.?)

13. If there was a policeman nearby, do you think you child would ask him for help if:
       He was lost and needed directions? _____
       He fell down and hurt himself? _____
       He saw a man with a gun walking down the street? _____
       He saw two people fighting and thought someone might get hurt?
       _____
       He saw someone running out of a bank with a bag of money? _____

14. How do you feel about the police?

15. Has child ever been to court with you? (yes/no)
    If yes: What was the occasion?
       How did he behave?
       Did he understand what was going on?
       Did he ask questions about the court?

Code Number _____

If no: Have you ever told him about being in court?
       Does he understand what happens in court?
       Has he ever asked you any questions about court?

*16. Does *child* know that you are in jail? (yes/no)
What was *child* told about where you were going?
Who told him?
Where does *child* think you are?
Does *child* know why you are gone/here? (yes/no)

**16. Does *child* know you are on probation? (yes/no)
What was *child* told about the sentence?
Does he know what you were charged with (or why you are on probation?)
(yes/no)
What do you think he understands about it?

*17. Do other people know that you are in jail? (yes/no) Neighbors? (yes/no)

**17. Do other people know that you are on probation? (yes/no) Neighbors? (yes/no)

*18. When someone asks *child* where you are, what does he tell them?

**18. When someone asks *child* about it, what does he tell them?

*19. Now, since you've been serving your sentence, who is your child living with?
Did *child* go to stay with _____ or did _____ come to
stay with *child*?

*20. Have the children stayed together or have they been separated from each other?
(together/separated)

*21. Did you make the arrangements for your child to stay there? (yes/no)
Was there a social worker, probation officer, or someone else who made the arrangements?

*22. Did you ask *child* about where he wanted to be while you were gone? (yes/no)

*23. What did *child* think or say about where he was going to stay, or who he was going to stay with?

*24. Have you seen your child since you've been here? (yes/no)
If yes: Has your child visited you here? (yes/no)
        If yes: How often has he visited? (_____ times)
                Would you tell me about the visit?
        If no: How did you get to see him?

*25. Do you want your child to visit you here? (yes/no)
How do you feel about having him visit you here?

*26. What do you think about the visiting conditions?
Could the visiting conditions be improved? (yes/no) Explain.

*27. Has *child* acted differently since you have been here? (yes/no)

Have you noticed any changes? (yes/no)
Could you describe what is different?
Has *child* acted any differently *toward you*?

**27. Has *child* acted differently since you've been on probation? (yes/no)
Have you noticed any changes?
Could you describe what is different?
Has *child* acted any differently *toward you*?

Let's look back to the time your child was growing up. Sometimes things come up so that a mother has to be separated from her children for a while, sometimes weeks or months or longer. For instance, if a mother has to go to the hospital, or her work schedule is bad, or she has been in jail.

28. Have you ever been separated from your child before? for a couple of days or more? (for jail mothers, not counting *this* time?) (yes/no)
If yes: How often have you been separated?
How long were the separations?
Could you tell me why you were separated before?
How old was *child* when the first separation occurred?
Does *child* remember you being gone before? (yes/no)
Where did he stay during those times? Who took care of him?
Did you know what was happening to *child* while you were gone? (yes/no) How did you find out?
Were there any problems during that separation for you or *child*?
What was it like when you and *child* got together again?
If no: So you have never been away from *child* for a couple days or more?

*29. How did *child* feel about you going away this time?
How did he act?

*30. Who is *child* closest to now that you aren't home with him?

**30. Who is *child* closest to now?

*31. Are you concerned that *child* might become attached to someone else while you are gone?

*32. Do you have any plans for your child's care after your release? (yes/no)
If yes: What are these plans?

*33. Will you live with your child when you get out?
Where will you live?

*34. Do you think there will be any problems when you get together again?

*35. Do you have any worries about how *child* will act toward you?

*36. What do you think will be the biggest problem for *you* when you get out?

*37. Have you been able to find out how your child(ren) are getting along?

Code Number _____

How do you find out? (Who?)
Have you talked to (*person who is taking care of child*) since you've been here?

*38. Have you talked to *child* on the telephone since you've been here? (yes/no)
If yes: How often?

*39. Have you written any letters to *child*? (yes/no)
If yes: How many?

Have you received any letters from *child* since you've been here?
If yes: How many?

*40. What keeps your child from visiting as often as allowed?

Child lives too far away _____
Lack of transportation _____
Lack of money _____
Child too young _____
Child does not want to visit _____
(Caretaker) won't permit *child* to visit _____
Mother does not want *child* to visit _____
Unsatisfactory visiting conditions _____
Other (specify) _____
_____

No obstacle, *child* visits often _____

41. I'd like to get some idea of the sort of rules you have for *child*. What are some of the things he is not allowed to do? (Do you have rules about bedtime, noise, time spent watching TV, homework, staying out at night, smoking, drugs, drinking, etc.?)

42. Are there things that *child* is supposed to do to help around the house? (yes/no)
If yes: What are his jobs?
Does he do them without being told, or do you have to keep after him to do them?

43. Do you have trouble getting *child* to mind you when you want him to do something? (yes/no)

44. When he's acting bad, do you ever tell him you are going to leave him?

45. Is there anybody *child* will listen to when he won't listen to you?

*46. When you are home, is *child* supposed to let you know where he is and what he is doing? (yes/no)

Does he do this?

**46. Is *child* supposed to let you know where he is and what he is doing? (yes/no)

Does he do this?

47. Suppose *child* skipped school, would you find out about it? (yes/no)

    Has this happened?
    What did (would) you do?
    If *child* gets in trouble at school, what do you do?

48. Would you tell me how *child* and his brother/sister get along together? (other children in the house?)

49. How does *child* get along with the neighbor children?

50. Do you know who his best friends are? (yes/no)
    If yes: What are their first names?

51. Has *child* ever been in trouble with the neighbors? (yes/no)
    With the police? (yes/no)
    With the school? (yes/no)
    If yes: What was the problem?

52. Could you tell me how you and *child* get along together?
    What sort of things do you enjoy about *child*?
    What does he do that gets on your nerves?

53. How do you punish *child*? Could you give me a couple examples?
    How does he act when you punish him?

54. What do you do when you are pleased with *child*, when he makes you happy?

55. Suppose you were doing something and *child* was bothering you? What happens? Can you describe a time like that? (For example, if you are watching something on TV and he wants to watch something else. What happens?)

56. How important is it to you for *child* to get good grades in school? How far would you like to see him go in school?
    Do you see his report card? (yes/no)
    What do you do when he has good grades? Do you say or do anything?
    What do you do when he has low grades?

57. Do you eat the evening meal together with *child*? (yes/no)
    How often?
    Is he talkative or quiet at meals?
    Do you eat breakfast with *child*? (yes/no)

58. Who does *child* go to when he's in trouble or feels unhappy, or doesn't he go to anyone in particular?

59. Do you think *child* takes after you in some ways?
    In what ways?

60. Who does *child* try to act like?

61. Compared to how you were raised as a child, are you doing about the same things with your child, or are you doing things differently?
What things are you doing the same? What things differently?

62. What is your greatest worry about your child?

To finish up the interview, I'd like to ask you some questions about yourself. Please remember that if I ask any questions you don't want to answer, just tell me so and we'll go to the next question.

1. How old are you?

2. What race or ethnic group are you?
____ White/Caucasian ____ Native American
____ Black ____ Asian-American
____ Mexican-American ____ Other

3. Do you have a religion? (yes/no)   What religion is it?_____

4. What was the last grade you finished in school?
Besides that, have you ever had any vocational training? (yes/no)
If yes: What kind of training?

5. Do you have a job now? (yes/no)
If yes: What kind of work are you doing? _____
Did you have a job at the time you were arrested? (yes/no)
If yes: Is it the same job you have now? (same/different)
If different: Why?

6. What kinds of jobs have you had most often?
What was the best job you ever had?
If you could have any job, what kind of job would you want?

7. Were you on welfare at the time you were arrested? (yes/no)
Now? (yes/no)
If no: As an adult, did you ever receive welfare, or aid to dependent children? (yes/no)

8. *Right now*, are you considered:
____ (1) legally married?
____ (2) common-law married/boyfriend?
____ (3) separated or divorced?
____ (4) deserted by husband?
____ (5) widowed?
____ (6) single, never married?

9. Have you ever been: (Check as many as apply.)
   _____ (1) legally married? (How many times?_____)
   _____ (2) common-law married/boyfriend?
   _____ (3) separated or divorced?
   _____ (4) deserted by your husband?
   _____ (5) widowed?
   _____ (6) never married?

10. Who did you live with or who lived with you: (Check as many as apply.)
    Just before you were arrested: **Now:**

    _____ (1) with legal husband   _____ (1)
    _____ (2) with common-law husband/boyfriend   _____ (2)
    _____ (3) with children   _____ (3)
    _____ (4) with other relatives   _____ (4)
    _____ (5) with friend(s)   _____ (5)
    _____ (6) alone   _____ (6)

11. If living with a man (#10):
    How long have you been living with him?
    Was he working at the time you were arrested? (yes/no)
    If yes: What kind of work was he doing?
    If no: What was the last kind of job he had?
           What was the last grade in school he finished?
           Has he ever been in jail or prison? (yes/no) What for?_____

12. What is your total number of dependents?
    How many people do you support?

13. While you were growing up, in how many places did you live; that is, how many
    times did you move?

14. Who raised you? (Were you raised by parents, relatives, foster homes?)

15. How many people were there in your family when you were growing up?

16. When you were a child, what type of job did your parents or the people you lived
    with work at most often?

17. When you were a child, would you say that your family or the people you lived with:
    _____ never had enough money?
    _____ had about enough money?
    _____ had more than enough money?

18. When you were a child, did your parent(s) or the people you lived with ever
    receive welfare, relief, or aid to dependent children? (yes/no)

19. Were you ever separated from *#14* for more than a couple of days while you were
    growing up? (yes/no)
    If yes: How often did that happen?
            How old were you?

How long was the separation?
What was the reason for the separtion?

20. Did anyone in your family ever spend time in jail or in prison? (yes/no)

    If yes: Who? _____

              When? _____

              What for? _____

21. Have any of your close friends ever been in jail or prison?

22. Did you ever go to juvenile court? (yes/no)

    If yes: What were you in juvenile court for?

              Did you spend time in juvenile hall or a camp or a home? (yes/no)

*23. As an adult, have you ever served time before? (yes/no)

    If yes: Jail or prison?

              How many times?

              What were you charged with?

**23. As an adult, have you ever served time? (yes/no)

    If yes: Jail or prison?

              How many times?

              What were you charged with?

24. How old were you when you were arrested for the first time?

*25. This time, what offense are you being held for?

**25. This time, what offense are you on probation for?

26. Were you already on probation at the time of this conviction? (yes/no)

    If yes: What were you on probation for?

27. Were your children involved in your offense? (yes/no)

    If yes: How? Crime partner or accessory? _____

                      Victim? _____

                      Other _____

28. Was anyone else involved with you? (yes/no)

    If yes: Who?

              Were they arrested?

              Were they convicted?

              Are they serving time or on probation?

29. Was your offense drug related? (yes/no)

    If yes: How?

              Were you addicted to drugs?

30. Was your offense alcohol related? (yes/no)

    Were you an alcoholic or a problem drinker?

31. Are you on any medication now? (yes/no)

    If yes: What are you taking?

              How much?

*32. How long is your sentence? _____ days.
     How long have you been here? (How much time served?)
     When do you expect to be released?

**32. How long is your probation?
      How long have you been on probation?
      When will it be finished?

*33. What is the hardest thing about being here for you?

**33. What is the hardest thing about being on probation for you?

*34. Is there anything about being here that is better than you had expected?

**34. Is there anything about being on probation that is better than you had expected?

Mothers' Interview
Time II

Code Number _____

Questions marked * to be asked *only* of jail mothers.
Questions marked ** to be asked *only* of probation mothers.
Questions not marked to be asked of both jail and probation mothers.

1. Children's names   Sex   Age

   _____   _____   _____
   _____   _____   _____
   _____   _____   _____
   _____   _____   _____
   _____   _____   _____

*2. What day did you get out?
    Is that when you expected to get out?
    Did you get "good time"?

*3. Where did you go when you first got out?

*4. When did you first see *child*?
    Where was that?
    Could you tell me what happened?
    How did you feel?
    How did *child* act?

5. Have there been any changes in where your child has been staying since the last
   time I talked with you? (yes/no)
   If yes: What was the change? Why was there a change?

6. Are you living in the same place as before, or have you moved?
   Who are you living with now?

7. Is *child* living with you now? (yes/no)
   If no: Where is *child*?
          Why is he there?
          Do you plan to live with him again sometime?
          If no: Why not?
          If yes: When will that be?

8. Who has legal custody of *child*?

*9. Are you on probation? (yes/no)
    If yes: For how long?

**10. Does *child* know you are on probation now? (yes/no)
     What was *child* told about the sentence?
     Does he know what you were charged with, or *why* you are on probation?
     What do you think he understands about it?

143

**11. Do other people know that you are on probation?
When someone asks *child* about it, what does he tell them?

**12. Did *child* ask you any questions or talk about the probation after the last interview we had? (yes/no)
What did you talk about?

*13. Does *child* talk about the time when you were gone?
What does *child* tell you about what happened when you were gone?
Does he talk about *caretaker*? What does he say about her?

*14. Has *child* asked you what it was like in jail? (yes/no)
If yes: What do you tell him?
If no: Do you ever talk to him about what it was like in jail?

*15. Does *child* tell other people, other kids or adults, that you've been in jail?
How do you feel about that?

*16. Is *child* worried that you will go away again and leave him?

*17. Who was *child* closest to when you were gone?

18. Who is *child* closest to now?

19. How is your child being supported now?
Are you receiving Aid to Dependent Children or some welfare support?

20. Are you working now? (yes/no)
If yes: What kind of work are you doing?
Is that the same job you had before you were arrested?
If no: Why?
If no: Are you looking for a job?

*21. What has been your biggest problem since you've been out?

*22. After I talked with you in jail, did *child* visit? (yes/no)
If yes: Could you tell me about the visit?
In the whole time you were in jail, did *child* visit? (never/once/____times)

*23. Did you find out how your *child* got along while you were gone? (yes/no)
If yes: From *caretaker*? _____ From *child*? _____

24. What school does *child* go to?
What grade is he in?
What is his teacher's name?

25. How is *child* doing in school?
Do you see his report card?

26. How does *child* get along with the neighbor children?
Do you know who his best friends are now?
What are their first names?

27. How are *child* and his brothers and/or sisters (or other children in the house) getting along?

    Are they fighting more or less than before you were arrested?

28. Have the police been to your house when *child* was home since the last time I saw you/since you were released? (yes/no)

    If yes: What were the circumstances? (To help in an emergency? To question you about something? To search the house? Earlier arrest? Called by you? Others?)

    Have *you* had any contact with the police since the last time I talked with you? (yes/no)

    If yes: Explain.

29. Do you know how *child* feels about policemen? (frightened, trusting, etc.)

30. If there was a policeman nearby, do you think your child would ask him for help if:

    a. He was lost and needed directions? ____
    b. He fell down and hurt himself? ____
    c. He saw a man with a gun walking down the street? ____
    d. He saw two people fighting and thought someone might get hurt? ____
    e. He saw someone running out of a bank with a bag of money? ____

31. How do *you* feel about the police now?

*32. Since you've been home, has *child* had any nightmares?
    Run away from home? Had other problems, eating, health, etc.?

33. Has *child* been in any trouble lately with the neighbors? (yes/no)
    With the police? (yes/no)
    At school? (yes/no)
    If yes: What was the problem?

34. Suppose *child* skipped school, would you find out about it?
    Has this happened?
    What did (would) you do?
    If *child* gets in trouble at school, what do you do?

35. Is *child* supposed to let you know where he is and what he is doing?
    Does he do this?

36. Are there things that *child* is supposed to do to help around the house?

37. Do you have trouble getting *child* to mind you when you want him to do something?

38. Is there anybody *child* will listen to when he won't listen to you?

39. When he's acting bad, do you ever tell him you are going to leave him?

40. Could you tell me how you and *child* are getting along together?
    What sort of things do you enjoy about him?
    What does he do that gets on your nerves?

41. How do you punish *child*? Could you give me a couple of examples? How does
    he act when you punish him?

To finish up the interview, I'd like to ask some questions about your experience with
the legal system and your attitudes.

1. Did you have a lawyer when you went to court? (yes/no)
    If yes: Public defender _____
            Private retained _____
            Legal assistance _____
    If no: Why not?

2. Do you think your lawyer was on your side? (yes/no)
    If you ever need a lawyer again, would you like to be represented by the same
    attorney? (yes/no) Why?

3. Did you have a trial or did you plead guilty?
    _____ Trial: with jury/without jury?
    _____ Pled guilty

4. Was there any deal or agreement made, that is, any plea bargaining that took
    place about the charge or the sentence? (yes/no)
    How did you feel about that?

5. What about the judge who sentenced you:
    Did he seem concerned about your welfare?/hostile to you/matter of fact?
    Did you get the feeling that the judge was neutral or that he was on one side or
    the other?
    Do you think the judge was fair? (yes/no)

6. Do you think the sentence you received was fair? (yes/no)

*7. Why do you think the judge sent you to jail instead of putting you on probation?

**7. Why do you think the judge put you on probation instead of sending you to jail?

I have a few questions about laws that I would like to get your opinion about. There
are obviously no right or wrong answers, but I would like your opinions.

8. What is a fair law?
    Why is it fair?
    Are all laws fair?

9. What would happen if there were no laws anywhere at all?
    Why?
    Why do we have rules and laws?

Code Number _____

10. Why should people follow laws?

11. Why do you follow laws?

12. Can laws be changed?
    If so, how can laws be changed?

13. If someone in charge told you to do something against the law, what would you
       do?
    Why?
    What should you do? Why?

14. Are there times when it might be right to break laws?
    When, if ever?
    Why do you feel this way?
    What does it mean to be right?

15. Can a person be right and break a law?
    How can this be?

16. Do you always get caught if you break a law?
    Why? How come?

17. What is a right?
    What kinds of rights should people have?

Child Interview

Code Number _____

Questions marked * to be asked of children of mothers in *jail only*.
Questions marked ** to be asked of children of mothers on *probation only*.
Questions not marked to be asked of all children.

Interview: I'm going to ask you some questions that I'd like you to answer. This isn't a test, but just some questions about things I'd like to know about you.

1. How old are you?

2. Are you a boy or girl?

3. What grade are you in? _____

4. What school do you go to now? _____

5. What is your teacher's name? _____

6. Do you have any brothers or sisters?
   What are their names? _____

*7. Who do you live with now?
    Why are you living here?
    How did you get here?
    Who brought you here?
    Did someone ask you if this is where you wanted to be? (yes/no)
       If yes: Who?
    Is this where you wanted to be? (yes/no)

**7. Who do you live with now?

*8. Who takes care of you?
    Did you ever stay with _____ before? (yes/no)
    Did you know _____ before you stayed here? (yes/no)

**8. Who takes care of you?
     How long have you lived here?

*9. How long has your mother been gone?

**9. How long have you lived here?
     (If child moved recently): Are you living near your same friends as before? (yes/no)
     If no: Have you made new friends?

*10. Do you know where your mother is?
     Where is she?
     Why is she there?
     When will your mother be back?

148

*11. Has your mother ever been away from home before? (yes/no)

If yes: How many times?
       Where did she go?
       How long was she gone?
       How old were you when she was away?
       What is it like when your mother is not at home?

*12. Are you in the same school as before your mother left?
Are you living near your same friends as before? (yes/no)

If no: Have you made new friends?

13. Who are your best friends? _____
Does your mother know who most of your friends are? (yes/no)
How does she usually act toward them?

*14. When your mother is at home, does she usually know where you are and what you are doing? (yes/no)
If yes: How does she know this?

**14. Does your mother usually know where you are and what you are doing? (yes/no)
If yes: How does she know this?

*15. Do your friends know that your mother is not at home?
Do they know where she is?
Where do your friends think your mother is?

*16. Does your teacher know where your mother is?

17. When someone asks you where your mother is, what do you tell them?

*18. Can you visit her? (yes/no)
If no: Why can't you visit her?

       Have you visited her (yes/no)
       If yes: When was that?

              What was it like when you visited her?
              Could you describe what happened?
              Do you want to visit her again? (yes/no)
              If no: Why not?

If no: Do you want to visit her? (yes/no)

*19. Can you talk to her on the telephone? (yes/no)
If no: Why can't you talk to her on the telephone?
If yes: Have you talked to her on the telephone?
       How often?

Do you want to talk to her on the telephone?

*20. Can you write letters to your mother? (yes/no)

Have you written a letter to her? (yes/no)
If yes: How many?

Do you want to write a letter to her? (yes/no)

Code Number _____

Have you gotten a letter from her? (yes/no)

*21. How do you like where you are living now?
How do you like living with _____?

*22. What is different about living with _____ than it was with your mother?

*23. Does your mother know what you are doing while she is away? (yes/no)
If yes: How does she know?

*24. What is it like when your mother is gone?
Is it hard for you? How?

*25. Have you gotten into trouble around here, at school or with the neighbors since she has been gone? (yes/no)
If yes: What kind of trouble?

**25. Have you gotten into any trouble with the neighbors, or at school lately? (yes/no)
If yes: What kind of trouble?

26. How do you and (*siblings*) get along together?
How do you get alone with the people you live with?

27. When your (parents) disagree about something, whose side are you usually on (your mother's or your father's)?

28. Who helps you when you have a problem?

29. Who do you get along with best of anybody you know?

30. Who do you want to be like when you get older?

31. Do you think you take after (or are like) your mother in some ways? (yes/no)
If yes: In what ways?

32. Who can tell you what to do and you do it?
(Who can make you do something you don't want to do?)

33. Has your mother ever been away from home for a couple of days or more? (yes/no)
If yes: How many times?
Where did she go?
How long was she gone?
How old were you when she was away?
What is it like when you mother is not at home?
Do you think your mother might go away again? (yes/no)
If yes: Why would she go away again?

34. Do you have any jobs to do around the house? (yes/no)
If yes: What jobs do you do?

35. Who do you usually eat dinner with?
Do you usually watch TV or talk, or is it quiet when you eat?

36. Who is it worst to be punished by?
    Why is it worst to be punished by _____?

37. Tell me how you feel about the police?
    Do you want to be a police officer when you are older? (yes/no)
    If yes: Why?   If no: Why not?

38. If you saw a policeman down the street, would you go ask for help or report it if:
    a. You were lost and needed directions? _____
    b. You fell down and hurt yourself? _____
    c. You saw a man with a gun walking down the street? _____
    d. Two grownups were fighting in your house and you thought someone might
       get hurt? _____
    e. You saw someone running out of a bank with a bag of money? _____

39. Have you ever gotten into any trouble with the police? (yes/no)
    If yes: What was it about?
            When was that?

40. Have you ever seen anybody get arrested? (yes/no)
    If yes: Who was it?
            Tell me what happened.

41. Does your mother have a social worker? (yes/no)
    If yes: What is her name?
            What does she say about your mother?

42. How do you like school?
    How are you doing in school?

*43. Does your mother see your report card from school? (yes/no)

**43. Does your mother see your report card from school when she is home? (yes/no)

*44. When will your mother come back again?
     If mother is *not* coming back, why won't she come back?
     Will you be together again?

*45. Where will you live when your mother comes back?
     Do you want to do that, or would you rather stay where you are now?

*46. What will things be like when your mother is home again?

47. What do you like to do most of all?
    What are you good at doing?

48. What makes you feel sad?
    What makes you feel happy?

1. What is a law?
   Why is that a law?

2. What is a fair law?
   Why is it fair?
   Are all laws fair? (yes/no)

3. What would happen if there were no laws anywhere at all? Why?
   Why do we have laws?

4. Why should people obey laws?

5. Why do you obey laws?

6. Can laws be changed? (yes/no)
   Why?   Why not?
   If yes: How can laws be changed?

7. If someone in charge told you to do something wrong, what would you do?
   Why?
   What should you do?   Why?

8. Are there times when it might be right to break laws? (yes/no)
   When, if ever?
   Why do you feel this way?
   What does it mean to be right?

9. Can a person be right and break a law? (yes/no)
   How can this be?

10. Do you always get caught if you break a rule?
    How come?

11. What is a right?

12. What kind of rights should a person have?

Questions Only for Child Who Knows Mother Is in Jail or on Probation

Code Number _____

1. Do you remember when your mother was arrested? (yes/no)
   Were you there? (yes/no)

   If yes: What happened?
   What did you do?
   How did you feel?
   What did the police do?
   Did the police talk to you? What did they say?
   Did the police use handcuffs?
   Did the police have guns?

   If no: How did you find out about it?
   Who told you?
   When did they tell you?
   What happened?
   What did the police do?

2. Do you know why your mother was arrested? (yes/no)
   Why do you think she was arrested?
   Did your mother break a rule or a law?

3. Do you know why your mother went to court? (yes/no) Why?

   Did you ever go to court with your mother? (yes/no)

   If yes: Tell me about that. What happened?

   If no: Do you know what happens in court? (yes/no)
   What?
   How do you know about courts?

   What does a judge do?
   What do lawyers do?

*4. Can you tell me why your mother is in jail? Can you explain?
   Do people always go to jail? Why do some people go to jail?

**5. Do you know what probation means? (yes/no)
   Can you tell me why your mother is on probation?
   Explain.
   Do people always get on probation (for doing that)?
   (Sometimes people go to jail: Why?)

*6. What do you think about your mother being in jail?
   Do you worry about her? (yes/no) What do you worry about?
   Is it hard on you to have your mother in jail? (yes/no)
   How is it hard?

153

Code Number _____

**6. What do you think about your mother being on probation?
Do you worry about her? (yes/no) What do you worry about?
Is it hard on you to have your mother on probation? (yes/no) How is it hard?

*7. Do your friends know that your mother is in jail? (yes/no)

**7. Do your friends know that your mother is on probation? (yes/no)

*8. Does your teacher know that your mother is in jail? (yes/no)

**8. Does your teacher know that your mother is on probation? (yes/no)

*9. Do you know what jails are like inside? (yes/no)
What is it like inside jail?

10. When someone asks you about what your mother did, what do you tell them?

Appendix B
Interviewer's
Introduction
to Mothers

Hello. My name is _____. I am a child researcher from Stanford University. I am not a part of the jail, probation department, or the courts or anything. I am trying to find out how children get along when they are separated from their mothers for some length of time. In order to do that I've been talking to mothers in jails, in halfway houses, and on probation. I am very concerned about what happens to children when their mothers are arrested and sentenced.

We don't know very much about the special problems that come up for both mothers and children when a mother goes to court—like what should the mother tell the child. Of course, mothers who are in jail have special problems about where the children will stay, where she should tell them she is going, and whether she should let the children visit. I would like to compare how things are going for mothers on probation who can stay home, with mothers in jail who must be separated from their children. I feel that if I could talk to some mothers about these sorts of things I could learn what they feel is important, if there are any problems, and how things are going for them. With this information from many mothers we hope that changes can be made to improve things, to help mothers know what to do with their children, and possibly to make changes in jail procedures.

Let me say just a couple of things. First, your answers are strictly confidential. I record them on this interview form, but this information is never given to anyone with your name on it. I use a code number instead of names.

I am going to ask a lot of questions. If you don't understand a question, or don't know what I mean, just ask me to explain. If I ask anything that you don't want to answer, just tell me and we'll go on to another question. If you want to discontinue the interview, just tell me and we'll stop. Do you have any questions?

I have a permission slip I'd like you to sign which says you agree to talk to me. I would also like to talk to your child. I will only talk with them if *you* give me your permission, and then only if *they* want to talk to me. They don't have to answer any questions that they don't want to. If your child does not know that you are in jail (on probation), I will not tell him and will just ask questions about how things have been lately. If you are uncertain about whether you want me to talk to your child, we can talk about that after your interview and you can decide about it then.

I would like to record this interview. That makes it easier for me to talk to you and to ask you questions than if I had to stop all the time to get everything down on paper, but if you prefer, I won't use the tape recorder.

I will say the date at the beginning of the tape so that I remember, but your name won't be on it. Will that be okay with you? No one in the jail (probation office) or welfare department or anything like that will ever hear these tapes or see your name. This information is strictly confidential and won't be given to anyone.

Remember, if I ask a question that you would rather not answer, just say so.

We are able to pay the mothers $25 for participating in the study. Payment is made upon completion of the second interview.

Appendix C
Sheriff's Letter of
Confidentiality
(Sample)

STANFORD UNIVERSITY
STANFORD, CALIFORNIA 94305

THE BOYS TOWN CENTER
FOR THE STUDY
OF YOUTH DEVELOPMENT

(415) 497-1706

Richard D. Hongisto, Sheriff
City Hall, Room 333
San Francisco, CA 94102

Dear Sheriff Hongisto:

I am writing in regard to "The Study of Children of Incarcerated Mothers" that is being conducted in the Bay Area, including San Francisco. To meet the requirements of the Stanford Committee on Human Subjects and in anticipation of possible LEAA funding to help underwrite some of the costs of the research project, I would like to reconfirm the confidentiality of the information obtained from the interviews of mothers in jail.

In compliance with the Crime Control Act of 1973 (P.L. 93-83), Guideline G 5400.2 provides policies pertaining to the rights and disposition of data. According to these guidelines no research or statistical data which is identifiable to any specific person and which has been furnished to the researcher by any agency or person in conjunction with this research shall be used or disclosed for any purpose other than the research project for which it was obtained. Pursuant to Section 524 (a), Public Law 93-83, such data is immune from legal process, and shall not, without the consent of the person furnishing such data, be admitted as evidence or used for any purpose in any action, suit or other judicial or administrative proceedings. Violation of these provisions can subject the researcher or any person making unlawful disclosures to a fine of up to $10,000.

This provision does not restrict the use of data in any interim or final research report, nor does it limit the distribution of such reports; it does, however, prohibit the researcher using or disclosing such research data identifiable to a specific person for any other purpose. As we initially agreed, your office will receive a copy of the final research report.

I would appreciate it if you would return one copy of this letter with your signature to acknowledge your concurrence.

If you have any questions or would like more information, please do not hesitate to contact me.

Sincerely,

Ann M. Stanton

157

Appendix D
Consent Forms

Mother's Consent Form

PERMISSION TO INTERVIEW

I agree to be interviewed for the purpose of the research project: A Study of Children of Incarcerated Mothers.

I understand that all information I may give is confidential. My participation is voluntary and I may discontinue the interview at any time.

I understand that if I am dissatisfied with any aspect of this program at any time, I may report grievances anonymously to the Sponsored Projects Office at Stanford University (497-2883).

Name:_____

Date:_____

Mother's Consent Form
for Child

PERMISSION TO INTERVIEW

I give permission for my child to be interviewed.
I also give permission for the researcher to contact
the school for information and records relating to
the child. All the information she receives will be
confidential.

Name:_____

Child's name

_____

_____

_____

Person taking care of the child:

_____

Address:

_____

_____

Phone:

_____

Child's Consent Form

PERMISSION TO INTERVIEW

I agree to be interviewed by Ann Stanton.

   I understand that any information I give will be confidential, that is, it will not be told to anyone else.

   I may end this interview at any time.

                         Name:_____

                         Date:_____

Appendix E
Release Form for
Probation Mothers

I agree to submit my name for consideration for the
research project--A Study of Children of Incarcerated
Mothers--that is being sponsored by the Boys Town
Center at Stanford University.

    I understand that I will be contacted and asked
whether or not I want to be interviewed. I understand
that if I agree to be interviewed that I may discontinue
the interview at any time. My participation will be
voluntary. Any information that I may give will be
confidential.

Name_____

Phone_____

Address_____

       _____

Ages of children_____

Date_____

Appendix F
Interviewer's
Clearance Letter
(Sample)

Office of the Sheriff

JOHN R. McDONALD, JR.
SHERIFF

HAROLD N. BARKER
ASSISTANT SHERIFF
OPERATIONS

MACDONALD U. CRAIK
ASSISTANT SHERIFF
ADMINISTRATION

COUNTY OF SAN MATEO

HALL OF JUSTICE AND RECORDS · REDWOOD CITY · CALIFORNIA 94063   TELEPHONE (415) 364-1811

ADDRESS ALL COMMUNICATIONS TO THE SHERIFF

August 20, 1975

To Whom It May Concern:

This letter will introduce Ms. Ann Stanton who is
conducting a Research Program for Stanford University.
Kindly allow her access to the women's jail at all
reasonable times. The authority of this letter expires
April 1, 1976.

Very truly yours,

JOHN R. McDONALD, JR., SHERIFF

Roger L. Goad, Leautenant
Commander, Main Jail

Appendix G
School Information Forms

Introductory Letter
to Schools

STANFORD UNIVERSITY
STANFORD, CALIFORNIA 94305

THE BOYS TOWN CENTER
FOR THE STUDY
OF YOUTH DEVELOPMENT

(415) 497-1706

To Whom it May Concern:

We are currently conducting a research study of mothers and
children in the Bay Area that is being sponsored by the Boys Town
Center for the Study of Youth Development at Stanford University.
A child in our study is enrolled in your school. A child's
school is contacted only if the mother has already agreed to
participate in the study, has been interviewed and has signed
consent forms granting permission for the child's school to be
contacted. We ask for your cooperation and assistance in collecting
the information necessary for the study.

Our usual procedure is to contact the principal of the school
the child is attending to describe the study and ask his/her
cooperation. A copy of the mother's signed consent form allowing
us to contact the school for information relating to the child is
available and may be retained for the child's file if desired. An
appointment is then made to meet with the child's classroom teacher
at the teacher's convenience. The meeting usually takes about 15
to 20 minutes of the teacher's time. We request information about
the child's attendance record, grades, achievement scores and
conduct, as indicated on the enclosed School Information Sheet. The
study does not involve any class time of the child, and we do not
request to personally see any of the child's school records.

Participation in the study by mothers and children has been
voluntary and the individuals have been assured of the confidentiality of the study. The confidentiality of the study prohibits
us from disclosing any information which is identifiable to a
specific person.

The child we are interested in obtaining information about
is _____. We would like descriptive
information prior to _____ and since that time.
Please make any additional comments that help explain the child's
situation or that describe the child in school.

Your cooperation and assistance are appreciated. Please call
the Boys Town Center if you have any questions or would like more
information.

Sincerely,

Ann M. Stanton

School Information

Student _____   Age _____

School _____   Height _____

Teacher _____   Weight _____

Grade _____   General Health _____

	Before	*Since*

Attendance
(days absent)
Explanation:

Deportment/
school behavior:

Average grades:

Class standing
(class rank):

Achievement level:
verbal/reading/math

Total number of
schools attended

Grades repeated _____

Grades skipped _____

Comments:

Behavior Rating Form

Student _____

School _____

Teacher _____

Grade _____

1. Does this child adapt easily to new situations, feel comfortable in new settings, enter easily into new activities?

____ always   ____ usually   ____ sometimes   ____ seldom   ____ never

2. Does this child hesitate to express his opinions, as evidenced by extreme caution, failure to contribute, or a subdued manner in speaking situations?

____ always   ____ usually   ____ sometimes   ____ seldom   ____ never

3. Does this child become upset by failures or other strong stresses as evidenced by such behaviors as pouting, whining, or withdrawing?

____ always   ____ usually   ____ sometimes   ____ seldom   ____ never

4. How often is this child chosen for activities by his classmates? Is his companionship sought for and valued?

____ always   ____ usually   ____ sometimes   ____ seldom   ____ never

5. Does this child become alarmed or frightened easily?
Does he become very restless or jittery when procedures are changed, exams are scheduled, or strange individuals are in the room?

____ always   ____ usually   ____ sometimes   ____ seldom   ____ never

6. Does this child seek much support and reassurance from his peers or the teacher, as evidenced by seeking their nearness or frequent inquiries as to whether he is doing well?

____ always   ____ usually   ____ sometimes   ____ seldom   ____ never

7. When this child is scolded or criticized, does he become either very aggressive (____) or very sullen and withdrawn (____)?

____ always   ____ usually   ____ sometimes   ____ seldom   ____ never

8. Does this child deprecate his schoolwork, grades, activities, and work products? Does he indicate he is not doing as well as expected?

____ always   ____ usually   ____ sometimes   ____ seldom   ____ never

9. Does this child show confidence and assurance in his actions toward his teachers and classmates?

____ always   ____ usually   ____ sometimes   ____ seldom   ____ never

10. To what extent does this child show a sense of self-esteem, self-respect, and appreciation of his own worthiness?

____ always   ____ usually   ____ sometimes   ____ seldom   ____ never

11. Does this child publicly brag or boast about his exploits?

____ always   ____ usually   ____ sometimes   ____ seldom   ____ never

12. Does this child continually seek attention, as evidenced by such behavior as speaking out of turn and making unnecessary noises?

____ always   ____ usually   ____ sometimes   ____ seldom   ____ never

Appendix H
Occupation Classification for Female Offenders

Major Group Classification	Subgroup Classifications
Professional	Teacher; librarian; dietician; home economist; RN (registered nurse); social worker; probation/parole officer; sociologist; psychologist
Managers, proprietors	Office manager; sales manager; store manager; proprietor of own shop/small business
Semiprofessional, technicians	Computer programmer; commercial artist; drafting; fashion designer; decorator; LVN (licensed vocational or practical nurse); health, medical technician/assistant; dental hygienist (note, except nurse aides, see personal services); airline stewardess, hostess; teacher's aide, recreation aide; counseling, community worker (not MSW); supervisor in factory, telephone company; armed forces
Skilled workers, craftsmen	Carpenter; painter; plumber; electrician; chef; baker; tailor, dressmaker (not in factory); upholsterer; barber; telephone installer; cutter (of apparel in factory)
Clerical workers	Secretary; typist; stenographer; bookkeeper; accounting clerk; keypunch operator; other office-machine operator (PBX, MTST); cashier; white-collar worker (works in office)
Sales workers	Sales clerk; insurance; real estate workers; stocks and bonds workers
Semiskilled workers	Bus driver; truck driver; taxi driver; cook, short order; electronics assembler; sewing-machine operator; blue-collar worker
Personal services	Beauty operator; cosmetologist; nurse aide; waitress; waiter; bartender; gardener; entertainers, legal; stripper; Go-Go girl, dancer; singer; model; masseur; sexual entertainers; prostitute; pimp; illegal nonsexual activities; bookie; pusher; dealer; thief; gambler
Unskilled workers	Maid; motel maid; laundry worker; sorter; carhop; dishwasher; cafeteria worker; cannery worker; farm worker; domestic; babysitter

Source: R.M. Glick and V.V. Neto, *National Study of Women's Correctional Programs*, Washington, D.C.: National Institute of Law Enforcement and Criminal Justice, 1977.

Appendix I
Summary Information on the Four County Jails

San Francisco County Jail #4 (San Bruno)

Capacity: 57   Actual number: 33
Year built: 1932   Security: medium
Design: single building in correctional complex
Living accommodations: 48 individual rooms, 1 dormitory
Cost per inmate: not available   Inmate/staff ratio: 2.4:1
Average time served: 6 months
Size of community: San Bruno, pop. 36,254
Distance to service area: 3-5 miles to San Bruno
Distance to metropolitan area: 15 miles to San Francisco, pop. 715,674
Public transportation: none within 5 miles

San Mateo County Jail

Capacity: 53   Actual number: 25
Year built: not available   Security: maximum
Design: 1 floor of single building
Living accommodations: 4 individual cells, 2 cells for 16 women,
                         1 drunk tank
Cost per inmate: not available   Inmate/staff ratio: 1.7:1
Average time served: 1 month
Size of community: Redwood City, pop. 55,688
Distance to service area: in service area
Distance to metropolitan area: 30 miles to San Francisco
Public transportation: within 2 blocks

Source: R.M. Glick and V.V. Neto, *National Study of Women's Correctional Programs*, Washington, D.C.: National Institute of Law Enforcement and Criminal Justice, 1977.

Alameda County Jail (Santa Rita)

Capacity: 140   Actual number: 85
Year built: not available   Security: medium
Design: one building in correctional complex
Living accommodations: 2 dormitories for 45 women each,
                         4 isolation cells, 6 cells for 6-8 women
Cost per inmate: $6,044   Inmate/staff ratio: 3.1:1
Average time served: 1 month
Size of community: Pleasanton, pop. 18,328
Distance to service area: 5 miles to downtown Pleasanton
Distance to metropolitan area: 30 miles to Oakland, pop. 361,561
Public transportation: none within 5 miles

Santa Clara County Jail (Elmwood)

Capacity: 133   Actual number: 82
Year built: not available   Security: medium &
                                                           maximum
Design: single building in correctional complex
Living accommodations: 22 individual cells, 2 dormitories, 1 drunk tank,
                         2 isolation cells, 2 padded cells,
                         2 cells for juveniles
Cost per inmate: not available   Inmate/staff ratio: 1.82:1
Average time served: not available
Size of community: Milpitas, pop. 32,400
Distance to service area: ½ mile
Distance to metropolitan area: 5-10 miles to San Jose
Public transportation: within 2-6 blocks

Appendix J
Rule-Law Interview

Name: _____

Instructions for Rule-Law Interview

This is part of a study on people's opinions and feelings about rules, obedience, and fairness. Different people have many different ideas on these topics. I want to know what you think; I want *your ideas*.

This is not a test. It has nothing to do with your marks in school. No one in school will see what you put down.

Be sure to answer every question. I am interested in finding out about your *ideas* and *reasons*. Therefore, please write down all the ideas and feelings the questions bring to mind rather than giving only "yes" and "no" answers.

Date _____

1. In recent years we have learned more and more about outer space. Imagine that people living on a planet like Mars came to visit Earth. If someone came from Mars and said to you, "Throw away one rule from anywhere. It can be a rule from your home, your school, or your country," what one rule would you throw away?

    Why?

2. Now imagine that we all went from Earth to Mars and started making rules, what would be the one best rule to make?

    Why?

3. What is a rule? Why is that a rule?

4. What is a law? Why is that a law?

5. If I asked you to close the window, is that a rule?

    Why?

    What is a request?

6. If I told you to close the window, is that a rule?

    Why?

    What is a command?

7. Why do we have rules and laws?

   What should rules and laws do?

   What do rules and laws do?

8. What does it mean for something to be fair?

9. Can some things be fair and right to do even when there are no rules and laws about them?

   How can this be?

10. What is a fair rule?

    Why is it fair?

    Are all rules fair?

11. What is a right?

12. What kinds of rights should people have?

    Why?

13. What kinds of rights do people have?

    Why?

14. What would happen if there were no rules anywhere at all?

    Why?

15. Why should people follow rules?

16. Why do you follow rules?

17. Can people in charge make you follow rules?

    Why?

18. Can rules be changed?

    Why?

    If so, how can rules be changed?

19. Can you do anything about changing rules?

    What?

20. If someone in charge told you to do something wrong, what would you do?

    Why?

    What should you do? Why?

21. If someone in charge told you to obey a bad rule, what would you do?

    Why?

    What should you do? Why?

22. Are there times when it might be right to break a rule?

    When, if ever?

    Why do you feel this way?

23. Do people obey because they have to? Why?

    Do people obey because they want to? Why?

24. What does it mean to be right?

25. Can a person be right and break a rule?

    How can this be?

26. What does it mean to be just?

27. Do you always get caught if you break a rule?

    Why? How come?

    Do people always get caught? Why?

28. After you have broken a bad rule, how do you feel?

    Why?

Appendix K
California Statute:
Female Prisoners—
Community Treatment
Programs

Chapter 1054; Assembly Bill no. 512

An act . . . to repeal Section 3401 of, and to add Chapter 4 (commencing with Section 3410) to Title 2 of Part 3 of, the Penal Code, relating to crimes.

Legislative Counsel's Digest

Existing law authorizes retention of children under 2 in the California Institution for Women if the mother is imprisoned there.

This bill would require the Department of Corrections to establish a community treatment program for such mothers and children who are eligible as specified.

The People of the State of California
Do Enact as Follows:

Sec. 2. The Legislature finds that the separation of infants from their mothers, while their mothers are in prison, can cause serious psychological damage to such infants. To alleviate the harm to such infants, consistent with the interest of public safety and justice, the following pilot program is enacted.

Sec. 3. Section 3401 of the Penal Code is repealed.

Sec. 4. Chapter 4 (commencing with Section 3410) is added to Title 2 of Part 3 of the Penal Code, to read:

Chapter 4. Community Treatment Programs

3410.
The term "community" shall, for purposes of this chapter, mean an environment away from the prison setting which is in an urban or suburban area.

3411.
The Department of Corrections shall on or before January 1, 1980, establish and implement a community treatment program under which

mother inmates who have one or more children under the age of two years and two months, whether born prior to or after January 1, 1978, shall be eligible to participate within the provisions of this section. The community treatment program shall provide for the release of the mother and child or children to a public or private facility in the community suitable to the needs of the mother and child or children, and which will provide the best possible care for the mother and child. In establishing and operating such program, the department shall have as a prime concern the establishment of a safe and wholesome environment for the participating children.

3412.

The Department of Corrections shall provide pediatric care consistent with medical standards and, to the extent feasible, shall be guided by the need to provide the following:

(a) A stable, care-giving, stimulating environment for the children as developed and supervised by professional guidance in the area of child development.

(b) Programs geared to assure the stability of the parent-child relationship during and after participation in the program, to be developed and supervised by appropriate professional guidance. These programs shall, at a minimum, be geared to accomplish the following:

(1) The mother's mental stability.

(2) The mother's familiarity with good parenting and housekeeping skills.

(3) The mother's ability to function in the community, upon parole or release, as a viable member.

(4) The securing of adequate housing arrangements after participation in the program.

(5) The securing of adequate child-care arrangements after participation in the program.

(c) Utilization of the least restrictive alternative to incarceration and restraint possible to achieve the objectives of correction and of this chapter consistent with public safety and justice.

3413.

In determining how to implement this chapter, the Department of Corrections shall be guided by the need to utilize the most cost-efficient methods possible. Therefore, the Director of Corrections may enter into contracts, with the approval of the Director of General Services, with appropriate public or private agencies, to provide housing, sustenance, and supervision for such inmates as are eligible for placement in community treatment programs. Prisoners in the care of such agencies shall be subject to all provisions of law applicable to them.

3414.

The department shall establish reasonable rules and regulations concerning the operation of the program.

3415.

(a) The probation department shall, on the day that any woman is sentenced to the state prison, notify such woman of the provisions of this chapter, if the term of the state imprisonment does not exceed two years on the basis of either the probable release or parole date computed as if the maximum amount of good time credit would be granted. The probation department shall determine such term of state imprisonment at such time for the purposes of this section.

(b) The woman may, upon the receipt of such notice, give notice of her desire to be admitted to a program under this chapter. The probation department or the defendant shall transmit such notice to the Department of Corrections, and to the appropriate local social services agency that conducts investigations for child neglect and dependency hearings.

3416.

If any woman received by or committed to the Department of Corrections has a child under two years of age, or gives birth to a child while an inmate under the jurisdiction of the Department of Corrections, such child and his or her mother shall, upon her request, be admitted to and retained in a community treatment program established by the Department of Corrections subject to the provisions of this chapter.

3417.

Subject to reasonable rules and regulations promulgated pursuant to Section 3414, the Department of Corrections shall admit to the program any applicant whose child was born prior to the receipt of the inmate by the department, if all of the following requirements are met:

(a) The applicant has a probable release or parole date with a maximum time to be served of two years, calculated after deduction of any possible good time credit.

(b) The applicant had no prior convictions for which she served a state prison term.

(c) The applicant was the primary caretaker of the infant prior to incarceration. If the infant was living with anyone other than the applicant and was receiving primary care from that person, the applicant is not eligible.

(d) At the date of the mother's application, the infant can not be older than:

If the applicant's release or parole date is:

2 months	2 years
8 months	16 months
18 months	5 1/3 months

(e) The applicant had not been found to be an unfit parent in any court proceeding, and the mother's fitness is not challenged pursuant to Section 3420 or she is found to be fit in a court proceeding. An inmate applicant shall not be denied the opportunity to participate in the program based in whole or in part on a determination that she is an unfit mother unless that decision is made pursuant to Section 232 of the Civil Code, Section 2625 of the Penal Code, or Section 600 of the Welfare and Institutions Code.

(f) Not more than 30 days has elapsed from the receipt of the mother by the Department of Corrections to the date of her application.

The Department of Corrections shall determine if the applicant meets the requirements of this section. The department may establish an appeal procedure for the applicant to appeal an adverse decision by the department. However, given the need to quickly place the child, the department's first determination shall govern the applicant's initial status as to these eligibility requirements.

3418.
In the case of any inmate who gave birth to a child after the date of sentencing, and in the case of any inmate who gave birth to a child prior to such date and meets the requirements of subdivisions (a), (b), and (d) of Section 3417 but has not yet made application for admission to a program, the department shall, upon the birth of the child, or the receipt of the inmate to the custody of the Department of Corrections, as the case may be, notify the inmate of the provisions of this chapter.

3419.
In the case of any inmate who gives birth after her receipt by the Department of Corrections, the department shall, subject to reasonable rules and regulations promulgated pursuant to Section 3414, upon her request, declare the inmate eligible to participate in a program pursuant to this chapter if all of the requirements of subdivisions (a), (b), (d), (e), and (f) of Section 3417 are met.

3420.
(a) Within five days after the receipt of an inmate by the Department of Corrections who has already applied for admission to a program, or of her application for admission to a program, whichever is later, the department shall give notice of her application to the child's current caretaker or guardian, if any, and if it has not already been notified pursuant to Section 3415, the appropriate local social services agency that conducts investigations for child neglect and dependency hearings.

(b) The department and the individuals and agencies notified shall have five days from the date of such notice to decide whether or not to challenge the mother's fitness. Lack of a petition filed by that time shall result in an assumption of the mother's fitness for the purposes of this chapter.

(c) The local agency which has been notified pursuant to Section 3415 shall not initiate the process of considering whether or not to file until after the sentencing court has sentenced the applicant to state prison.

(d) The appropriate local agency that conducts investigations for child neglect and dependency hearings, the Department of Corrections, and the current guardian or caretaker of the child, shall have the authority to file for a fitness proceeding against the mother after the mother has applied in writing to participate in the program.

(e) The determination of whether or not to file shall be based in part on the likelihood of the mother being a fit parent for the child in question both during the program and afterwards. Program content shall be taken into account in this determination. There shall be a presumption affecting the burden of producing evidence in favor of filing for a fitness proceeding under the following circumstances:

(1) The applicant was convicted of one or more of the following violent felonies:

(i) Murder.

(ii) Mayhem.

(iii) Kidnapping as defined in Section 207 or 209.

(iv) Lewd acts on a child under 14 as defined in Section 288.

(v) Any other felony in which the defendant inflicts great bodily injury on a person other than accomplices which has been alleged and proven.

(vi) Forceable rape in violation of subdivision (2), (3), or (4) of Section 261.

(vii) Sodomy by force, violence, duress, menace, or threat of great bodily injury.

(viii) Oral copulation by force, violence, duress, menace, or threat of great bodily injury.

(2) The applicant was known to be addicted to any drug immediately prior to the date of her crime leading to the prison sentence, and the mother is not under the care of a doctor who has prescribed such drug.

(3) The applicant was convicted of child abuse in the current or any proceeding.

(f) Fitness petitions shall be resolved in the court of first instance as soon as possible for purposes of this section. Given the need to place the child as soon as possible, the first determination by the court as to the applicant's fitness as a mother shall determine her eligibility for the program for the current application. Outcomes of appeals shall not affect eligibility.

3421.

Children of women inmates may only participate in the program until they reach the age of two years and two months, at which time the Community

Release Board may arrange for their care elsewhere under any procedure authorized by statute and transfer the mother to another placement under the jurisdiction of the Department of Corrections if necessary; and provided further, that at its discretion in exceptional cases, including, but not limited to, cases where the mother's period of incarceration is extended, the board may retain such child and mother for a longer period of time.

3422.

The costs for care of any mother and child placed in a community treatment program pursuant to this section shall be paid for out of funds allocated to the department in the normal budgetary process. The department shall make diligent efforts to procure the allocation of sufficient funds and shall limit its use of the General Fund to meet the matching fund requirements of other funding sources. However, in no event shall General Fund moneys exceed 25 percent of the overall costs of the project.

3423.

Any woman inmate who would give birth to a child during her term of imprisonment may be temporarily taken to a hospital outside the prison for the purposes of childbirth, and the charge for hospital and medical care shall be charged against the funds allocated to the institution. The board shall provide for the care of any children so born and shall pay for their care until suitably placed, including, but not limited to, placement in a community treatment program.

3424.

On or before March 30, 1980, and on or before March 30, 1981, the Department of Corrections shall evaluate the cost efficiency and effect of this chapter and shall report back to the Legislature with the department's recommendations as to whether or not this chapter should be altered or repealed and if so, why.

Approved Sept. 23, 1978.

Filed Sept. 25, 1978.

Appendix L
Uniform Law
Commissioners Model
Sentencing and
Corrections Act

Section 4-1116. [Preserving Parental Relationships.]
(a) The director shall:

(1) assist confined persons in (i) communicating with their children and otherwise keeping informed of their affairs, and (ii) participating in decisions relating to the custody, care, and instruction of their children; and

(2) provide any confined person or any person accused of an offense access to relevant information about child-care facilities available in the department, counseling, and other assistance in order to aid the person in making arrangements for his child.

(b) The director may:

(1) establish and maintain facilities or parts of facilities suitable for the care and housing of confined persons with their children;

(2) authorize periodic extended or overnight visits by children with a confined person;

(3) authorize a child, upon the request of the confined person, to reside with the person in a facility while the person is entitled to custody of the child or if the person gives birth to the child during confinement.

(c) In determining whether a child may reside in a facility or visit a facility on an extended or overnight basis pursuant to subsection (b), the following factors, among others, must be considered:

(1) the best interest of the child and the confined person;

(2) the length of sentence imposed on the confined person and the likelihood that the child could remain in the facility throughout the confined person's term;

(3) the nature and extent of suitable facilities within the department;

(4) available alternatives that would protect and strengthen the relationship between the child and the confined person; and

(5) the age of the child.

(d) A child may not reside in a facility or visit a facility on an extended or overnight basis if:

(1) the division of correctional medical services certifies that the confined person is physically or emotionally unable to care for the child;

(2) the [Department of Welfare] certifies that the conditions in the facility will result in a substantial detriment to the physical or emotional well-being of the child; or

(3) the [juvenile, family court] orders that the child not do so.

(e) Whenever a child is authorized to reside in a facility or visit a facility on an extended or overnight basis, the director shall provide for the child's basic needs including food, clothing, and medical care if the confined person is unable to do so. The department is subrogated to any rights the confined person has against any other person or organization on account of those expenses.

(f) Whenever the director allows a child to reside with a confined person in a facility he shall notify the [Department of Welfare] which may take any action authorized by law to protect the best interest of the child.

(g) This section does not limit or otherwise affect the power of a court to determine the nature and extent of parental rights of confined persons or to determine the custody of children.

Comment

One of the serious side effects of confining persons convicted of crimes is the resulting destruction of family relationships. P. Morris, *Prisoners and Their Families* (1965). It has long been recognized that the existence of a supportive relationship is one of the few factors that can be shown statistically to have an affirmative influence on recidivism. See D. Glaser, The Effectiveness of a Prison and Parole System 378-80; (1964) (relating residence with wife after release to postrelease success); Holt & Miller, *Explorations in Inmate-Family Relationships* (1972) (relating extent of visitation to parole success); N. Morris, *The Future of Imprisonment* 35 (1974).

The importance of preserving family relationships has been recognized in ABA Joint Comm., §6.2; ACA Manual at 542 ("As a matter of general policy, the members of the inmate's family should be permitted and encouraged to maintain close contact with the inmate, not only to help his morale while serving a sentence but to sustain family life, ensure close ties after release, and assist in the inmate's institutional adjustment, giving him encouragement and helping him keep in touch with the outside world in a practical way."); Nat'l Advisory Comm'n Correc. Std. 2.17.

Various studies indicate a large percentage of women prisoners have children. See Singer, Women and the Correctional Process, 11 Am. Crim. L. Rev. 295, 302 (1973) (reporting the findings of four studies which show the following percentage of women prisoners have children: California (50%), federal system (70%), Pennsylvania (80%), and District of Columbia (86%). See also Note, The Prisoner-Mother and Her Child, 1 Cap. U. L. Rev. 127 (1972). A 1971 study disclosed that in the year 239 babies were born to prisoners in state institutions. E. Chandler, Women in Prison 118-19 (1973). Figures indicating children affected by the imprisonment of men are even less available. It is reported that in one year in Oregon, "774 men newly committed for felonies left behind a total of 988 children." Sack, Seidler, & Thomas, The Children of Imprisoned Parents: A Psychosocial Exploration, 46 Am. J. Orthopsychiat. 618 (1976).

There are no specific figures on how many children are being retained in correctional institutions to be with their parents. The 1970 census lists 53 children under the age of 5 in correctional institutions and another 60 in local jails and workhouses. The census also shows 67 children between the age of 5 and 9 in prison and 76 in local jails. These children are distinguished from those living in training schools for juvenile delinquents and thus it is unlikely that they are in correctional institutions as a result of their own criminal activity. U.S. Dept. of Commerce Bureau of Census, Persons in Institutions and Other Group Quarters, Table 3, at 5 (1973).

The traditional official response to the problem of the children of confined persons is to place them with other individuals or agencies with or without the permission of the confined parent. In many jurisdictions conviction of serious offenses is a ground for termination of parental rights. See generally, Project, The Collateral Consequences of a Criminal Conviction, 23 Vand L. Rev. 929, 1074-1079, (1970) (providing a survey of state provisions).

Many states have no specific provision relating to children of prisoners. Those states that have addressed the problem have taken a variety of courses. Cal. Penal Code, §3401 (West 1970) (allows child to remain until two years of age when board of corrections arranges for its care elsewhere); Fla. Stat. Ann., §944.24 (West 1973) (allows child to be retained in institution for eighteen months and longer in exceptional cases); Me. Rev. Stat. Ann. tit. 34, §815 (West Supp. 1976-1977) (custody of child determined "at instance of the department" in accordance with procedure for divesting parents of neglected children of their parental rights); Mass. Gen. Laws Ann. ch. 127, §142 (West 1974) (authorizes parole of pregnant prisoners); N.Y. Correc. Law, §6.11 (McKinney 1968) (gives mother the right to bring child into institution until child is 1 year old unless the mother is physically unfit to care for child or not in the child's best interest). See also Apgar v. Beauter, 75 Misc. 2d 439, 347 N.Y.S.2d 872 (1973), holding the jailer did not have a right to arbitrarily deny the mother the right to retain her child in the jail:

> It is a general and well-established principle in this state that the welfare of a child is best served by remaining with its natural parent. . . . That incarceration in a jail or correctional institution per se does not constitute such unfitness or exceptional circumstances so as to require that a newborn infant be taken from its mother is attested to by the enactment by the Legislature of subdivision 2 of section 611 of the Correction Law. In fact, it has been New York's policy for over 40 years to permit inmate mothers to keep their newborn infants. . . . So important does the Legislature consider the natural mother-child relationship that even the father does not

have the power under this statute to countermand the decision of an inmate mother to keep her child. *Id.* at 440-41, 347 N.Y.S.2d at 875.

The problem of children of confined persons involves a delicate balancing of the parent's interest, the child's interest, and the state's interest in administering correctional facilities. The parents' interest in preserving the relationship is clear. The state's interest is mixed—in many cases preserving the relationship may reduce recidivism but contemporary prisons are unsuited for raising children. The child's interest may also be mixed; although a prison is not an ideal environment for children, the child does benefit from continuity and stability in his relationship with his parent and some tentative findings suggest that children, particularly those in puberty, who are separated from their parent because of the latter's incarceration, exhibit a higher incidence of antisocial behavior. See Sack, Seidler, & Thomas, supra; Sack, Children's Reactions to the Imprisonment of Their Parents (Paper presented to the 1976 Annual Meeting of the American Academy of Child Psychiatry). The thrust of this section is to facilitate the continuation of the parent-child relationship within a prison context if necessary and appropriate. For additional psychological and legal support for this section, see Note, On Prisoners and Parenting: Preserving the Tie That Binds, 87 Yale L.J. 1408 (1978).

Subsection (a) authorizes the director to assist confined persons in maintaining their parental relationships. He is required to assist confined persons in communicating with their children and, to the extent they are able, to participate in decisions affecting their children. The decisions to which this section is directed include both formal decisions made by a child-care agency or a juvenile court and informal decisions made by temporary guardians. To the extent that confinement permits, the confined parent should be allowed to counsel or otherwise direct the upbringing of his children unless formal legal proceedings have terminated his right to do so.

Subsection (b) authorizes, but does not require, the director to permit extended overnight visits by children or to permit children to reside with their parents in a facility and to make appropriate provision for them. A variety of factors, provided in subsection (c), would influence a decision to allow permanent residence by children in a facility. No statutory restrictions on this authority are provided because of the complex mixture of factors which often exist. In most instances, it is likely that only very young children would be allowed to remain for limited periods of time with their parents in confinement. However, in a half-way house or other community-based facility and with parents with very short terms, it may be appropriate and beneficial to include older children.

Subsection (d) provides for some external review by the division of medical services, the department of welfare, and the juvenile or family court in order to protect the interests of the child.

Subsection (e) authorizes the expenditure of departmental funds to provide for the basic needs of children visiting or residing in a facility. The section is drafted to emphasize that the confined parent must pay for these basic provisions unless he is unable to do so. The last sentence of the subsection is intended to allow the department to seek, by way of subrogation funds available for the care of children. This would authorize the department to seek enforcement of a child-support order against a spouse of a confined person where the department provides basic support to the child.

Subsection (f) enhances the external review by the department of welfare or other agency generally concerned with the care and custody of parentless children. The last phrase of the subsection is intended to incorporate any existing state provision for protecting the child's interest such as procedures authorizing the appointment of a guardian ad litem.

Subsection (g) ensures that the authority granted by this section is subordinate to the power of any court to determine parental rights or child custody.

Bibliography

Adelson, J., and Beall, L. 1970. "Adolescent Perspectives on Law and Government." *Law and Society Review* 4 (May):495-504.

Adelson, J., Green, B., and O'Neil, R. 1969. "Growth of the Idea of Law in Adolescence." *Developmental Psychology* 1 (4):327-332.

Ainsworth, M.D. 1966. "The Effects of Maternal Deprivation: A Review of Findings and Controversy in the Context of Research Strategy." In *Deprivation of Maternal Care: A Reassessment of Its Effects*. New York: Schocken Books. Originally published, Geneva: World Health Organization, 1962.

Ainsworth, M.D., and Bell, S.M. 1970. "Attachment, Exploration, and Separation: Illustrated by the Behavior of One-Year-Olds in a Strange Situation." *Child Development* 41:49-67.

American Association of University Women. 1969. *Report on the Survey of 41 Pennsylvania County Court and Correctional Services for Women and Girl Offenders*. Philadelphia: American Association of University Women, Pennsylvania Division.

American Bar Association. 1976. *Female Offenders: Problems and Programs*. Washington, D.C.: Female Offender Resource Center.

Bandura, A., and Walters, R.H. 1963. *Social Learning and Personality Development*. New York: Holt, Rinehart and Winston.

Barry, E. 1979. "Legal Services Available to Incarcerated Parents and Their Children: Survey and Analysis." Paper presented at the Conference on Incarcerated Parents and Their Children. National Institute of Mental Health, Bethesda, Maryland.

Baunach, P.J. 1979. "The Families of Inmate Mothers: Perceptions of Separation from Their Children." Paper presented at the Conference on Incarcerated Parents and Their Children. National Institute of Mental Health, Bethesda, Maryland.

Black, M. 1979. "A Prototype Project: Services for Incarcerated Mothers and Their Children at the Women's Residential Center, Santa Clara County Sheriff's Department." Paper presented at the Conference on Incarcerated Parents and Their Children. National Institute of Mental Health, Bethesda, Maryland.

Blackwell, J.E. 1959. "The Effects of Involuntary Separation on Selected Families of Men Committed to Prison from Spokane County, Washington." Doctoral dissertation, State College of Washington.

Bonfanti, M.A., Felder, S.S., Loesch, M.L., and Vincent, N.J. 1974. "Enactment and Perception of Maternal Role of Incarcerated Mothers." Masters thesis, Louisiana State University.

Botler, S. 1979. "A General Description of Legal Problems Facing the Incarcerated Parent with Respect to His/Her Child." Paper presented at
the Conference on Incarcerated Parents and Their Children. National
Institute of Mental Health, Bethesda, Maryland.

Bouma, D.H. 1969. *Kids and Cops.* Grand Rapids, Mich.: Eerdmans.

Bowlby, J. 1946. *Forty-Four Juvenile Thieves: Their Characters and Home
Life.* London: Bailliere, Tyndall & Cox.

_____ . 1966. *Maternal Care and Mental Health.* New York: Schocken
Books. Original edition, 1951.

_____ . 1973. *Attachment and Loss, Volume II: Separation.* New York:
Basic Books.

Burger, W. 1970. "Address at the American Bar Association Annual Convention." *The New York Times.* August 11, p. 24.

Burkhart, K.W. 1971. "Women in Prison." *Ramparts* (June):21-29.

_____ . 1973. *Women in Prison.* Garden City, N.Y.: Doubleday and Co.

Burlingham, D., and Freud, A. 1942. *Young Children in War-Time.* London: Allen and Unwin.

_____ . 1944. *Infants without Families.* London: Allen and Unwin.

Cain, A.C., and Fast, I. 1966. "Children's Disturbed Reactions to Parent
Suicide." *American Journal of Orthopsychiatry* 36 (5):873-880.

Cappeller, V.J. 1972. "Stigma in the Lives of Psychiatric Hospital
Patients and Their Families with Special Reference to Their Children."
Doctoral dissertation, Brandeis University.

Casper, J.D. 1972. *American Criminal Justice: The Defendant's Perspective.* Englewood Cliffs, N.J.: Prentice-Hall.

Chandler, E.W. 1973. *Women in Prison.* Indianapolis: Bobbs-Merrill.

Chapman, A.W. 1956. "Attitudes toward Legal Authorities by Juveniles:
A Comparative Study of Delinquent and Nondelinquent Boys."
Sociology and Social Research (June):170-175.

Cloninger, C.R., and Guze, S.B. 1970. "Female Criminals: Their Personal,
Familial and Social Backgrounds." *Archives of General Psychiatry*
23:554-558.

Contact, Inc. ed. 1978. *Woman Offender.* Lincoln, Nebraska: Contact
Publications.

Coopersmith, S. 1967. *The Antecedents of Self-esteem.* San Francisco:
W.H. Freeman and Company.

Daehlin, D., and Hynes, H. 1974. "A Mother's Discussion Group in a
Women's Prison." *Child Welfare* 53 (7):464-470.

Damon, W. 1977. *The Social World of the Child.* San Francisco: Jossey-
Bass Publishers.

DeFord, M.A. 1962. *Stone Walls: Prisons from Fetters to Furloughs.*
Philadelphia: Chilton.

Despert, J.L. 1962. *Children of Divorce.* Garden City, N.Y.: Doubleday
and Co. Originally published, 1953.

Douglas, J.W.B., Ross, J.M., and Simpson, H.R. 1968. *All Our Future: A Longitudinal Study of Secondary Education.* London: Peter Davis.

Eyman, J.S. 1971. *Prisons for Women.* Springfield, Ill.: Charles C. Thomas.

Friedman, S., and Esselstyn, T.C. 1965. "The Adjustment of Children of Jail Inmates." *Federal Probation* 29:55-59.

Giallombardo, R. 1966. *Society of Women: A Study of Women's Prisons.* New York: John Wiley & Sons.

Gibbs, C. 1971. "The Effect of the Imprisonment of Women upon Their Children." *British Journal of Criminology* 11 (2):113-130.

Gibson, H.B. 1969. "Early Delinquency in Relation to Broken Homes." *Journal of Child Psychology and Psychiatry* 10:195-204.

Glaser, D. 1964. *The Effectiveness of a Prison and Parole System.* Indianapolis: Bobbs-Merrill.

Glick, R.M. and Neto, V.V. 1977. *National Study of Women's Correctional Programs.* Washington, D.C.: National Institute of Law Enforcement and Criminal Justice.

Glueck, S., and Glueck, E.T. 1934. *500 Delinquent Women.* New York: Alfred A. Knopf.

_____ . 1950. *Unraveling Juvenile Delinquency.* Cambridge, Mass.: Harvard University Press.

Goldstein, J., Freud, A., and Solnit, A.J. 1973. *Beyond the Best Interests of the Child.* New York: Free Press.

_____ . 1979. *Before the Best Interests of the Child.* New York: Free Press.

Grant, W.M., LeCornu, J., Pickens, J.A., Rivkin, D.H., and Vinson, C.R. 1970. "The Collateral Consequences of a Criminal Conviction." *Vanderbilt Law Review* 23 (5):929, 1074-1079.

Greenstein, F.I. 1965. *Children and Politics.* New Haven, Conn.: Yale University Press.

Groves, E.R. 1952. *The Family and Its Social Problems.* Chicago: University of Chicago Press.

Hess, R.D., and Torney, J.F. 1967. *The Development of Political Attitudes in Children.* Chicago: Aldine Publishing Co.

Hetherington, E.M., Cox, M., and Cox, R. 1975. "Beyond Father Absence: Conceptualization of Effects of Divorce." Paper presented at the Meetings of the Society for Research in Child Development, Denver.

_____ . 1976. "The Aftermath of Divorce." Paper presented at meetings of the American Psychological Association, Washington, D.C.

Hill, R. 1949. *Families under Stress.* New York: Harper and Bros.

Hinde, R.A., and Spencer-Booth, Y. 1971. "Effects of Brief Separation from Mother on Rhesus Monkeys." *Science* 173:111-118.

Hollingshead, A.B. 1957. "Two Factor Index of Social Position." Unpublished manuscript. (Available from 1965 Yale Station, New Haven, Connecticut.)

Holt, N., and Miller, D. 1972. "Explorations in Inmate-Family Relationships." Research Report no. 46. Sacramento, Calif.: Department of Corrections.

Johnson, E.H. 1969. "Childbirth to Women under Sentence: Characteristics and Outcome." Unpublished manuscript. Carbondale, Ill.: Southern Illinois University Center for the Study of Crime, Delinquency and Corrections.

Junior League of the City of New York. 1974. *Junior League Report: A Prison Nursery Study*. New York: Junior League.

Kohlberg, L. 1964. "Development of Moral Character and Moral Ideology." In M.L. Hoffman and L.W. Hoffman, eds. *Review of Child Development Research*, vol. 1. New York: Russell Sage Foundation.

———. "Stage and Sequence: The Cognitive-Developmental Approach to Socialization." In D. Goslin, ed. *Handbook of Socialization Theory and Research*. Chicago: Rand McNally College Publishing Co.

Kohlberg, L., and Freundlich, D. 1973. "Moral Judgment in Youthful Offenders." In L. Kohlberg and E. Turiel, eds. *Moralization: The Cognitive Developmental Approach*. New York: Holt, Rinehart and Winston.

Koontz, B. 1971. "Public Hearings on Women and Girl Offenders." D.C. Commission on the Status of Women, November 4. Washington, D.C.: U.S. Department of Labor.

Landauer, T.K., Carlsmith, J.M., and Lepper M. 1970. "Experimental Analysis of the Factors Determining Obedience of Four-Year-Old Children to Adult Females." *Child Development* 41:601-611.

LaPoint, V., and Radke-Yarrow, M. 1979. "Imprisoned Mothers and Their Children: Affective and Social Dimensions of Their Relationships." Paper presented at the Conference on Incarcerated Parents and Their Children, National Institute of Mental Health, Bethesda, Maryland.

Lundberg, D., Sheekley, A., and Voelker, T. 1975. "An Exploration of the Feelings and Attitudes of Women Separated from Their Children due to Incarceration." Masters practicum, Portland State University.

Maas, H.S. 1963. *The Young Adult Adjustment of Twenty Wartime Residential Nursery Children*. New York: Child Welfare League of America, Inc.

Maccoby, E.E. 1968. "The Development of Moral Values and Behavior in Childhood." In J.A. Clausen ed. *Socialization and Society*. Boston: Little, Brown and Company.

Maccoby, E.E., and Feldman, S.S. 1972. "Mother-attachment and Stranger-reactions in the Third Year of Life." *Monograph of the Society for Research in Child Development*, no. 1, vol. 37.

McCord, J., and McCord, W. 1958. "The Effects of Parental Role Model on Criminality." *Journal of Social Issues* 14:66-75.

McCord, W., McCord, J., and Zola, I.K. 1959. *Origins of Crime: A New Evaluation of the Cambridge-Somerville Youth Study*. New York: Columbia University Press.

McDermott, J.F. 1970. "Divorce and Its Psychiatric Sequelae in Children." *Archives in General Psychiatry* 23:421-427.

McGowan, B.G., and Blumenthal, K.L. 1978. *Why Punish the Children? A Study of Children of Women Prisoners*. Hackensack, N.J.: National Council on Crime and Delinquency.

McWhinnie, J.B. 1961. *Denmark: A New Look at Crime*. London: Stevens & Sons.

Markley, C.W. 1973. "Furlough Programs and Conjugal Visiting in Adult Correctional Institutions." *Federal Probation* 37:19-26.

Martin, J.P., and Webster, D. 1971. *The Social Consequences of Conviction*. London: Heinemann.

Miller, D., Challas, G., and Gee, S. 1972. "Children of Convicts: A Fifteen Year Follow-up Study, 1956-1971." San Francisco: Scientific Analysis Corporation.

Moerk, E.L. 1973. "Like Father Like Son: Imprisonment of Fathers and the Psychological Adjustment of Sons." *Journal of Youth and Adolescence*, no. 2, vol. 4.

Monahan, F. 1941. *Women in Crime*. New York: I. Washburn, Inc.

Morris, N. 1974. *The Future of Imprisonment*. Chicago: University of Chicago Press.

Morris, P. 1965. *Prisoners and Their Families*. New York: Hart Publishing Co.

Musk, H. 1979. "Incarcerated Women and Their Children: Preliminary Report #1." Jessup, Md.: Association of Programs for Female Offenders, Maryland Correctional Institution for Women.

National Institute of Law Enforcement and Criminal Justice, U.S. Department of Justice. 1979. Uniform Law Commissioners' Model Sentencing and Corrections Act.

Note. 1978. "On Prisoners and Parenting: Preserving the Tie That Binds." *Yale Law Journal* 87:1408.

Owens, C. 1979. "Families of Black Offenders: Relationships with Their Extended Family." Paper presented at the Conference on Incarcerated Parents and Their Children, National Institute of Mental Health, Bethesda, Maryland.

Palmer, D. 1972. "The Prisoner-Mother and Her Child." *Capital University Law Review* 1:127-144.

Perlman, H.S. 1979. "Incarcerated Parents and Their Children—The Uniform Law Commissioners' Model Sentencing and Corrections Act." Paper presented at the Conference on Incarcerated Parents and Their Children, National Institute of Mental Health, Bethesda, Maryland.

Piaget, J. 1965. *The Moral Judgment of the Child*. New York: Free Press. Originally published, 1932.

Portune, Robert G. 1966. *Attitudes of Junior High School Pupils toward Police Officers*. Cincinnati: University of Cincinnati.

Reeves, M. 1929. *Training Schools for Delinquent Girls*. New York: Russell Sage Foundation.

Rutter, M. 1972. *Maternal Deprivation Reassessed*. Middlesex, England: Penguin Books.

Sack, W.H. 1976. "Children's Reactions to the Imprisonment of Their Parents." Paper presented to 1976 Annual Meeting of American Academy of Child Psychiatry.

_____ . 1977. "Children of Imprisoned Fathers. *Psychiatry*. 40(2):163-174.

Sack, W.H., Seidler, J., and Thomas, S. 1976. "The Children of Imprisoned Parents: A Psychosocial Exploration." *American Journal of Orthopsychiatry* 46(4):618-628.

Santa Clara County Proposal: Women's Residential Center Program. 1975. Santa Clara County, California.

Savage, J. 1979. "Separation and Its Effects on Female Prisoners and Their Children." Paper presented at the Conference on Incarcerated Parents and Their Children, National Institute of Mental Health, Bethesda, Maryland.

Schiff, E.J. 1965. "The Effects upon Children of Hospitalization of Their Parents." *Child Welfare* 44(6):305-310.

Singer, L.R. 1973. "Women and the Correctional Process." *American Criminal Law Review* 11:295, 302.

Skoler, D.L., and McKeown, J.C. 1974. "Women in Detention and State-wide Jail Standards." Washington, D.C.: American Bar Association Commission on Correctional Facilities and Services.

Smith, A.D. 1962. *Women in Prison: A Study in Penal Methods*. Stevens & Sons.

Soares, C.M., and Soares, A.T. 1969. "Social Learning and Social Violence." *Proceedings*. 77th Annual Convention of the American Psychological Association. Washington, D.C.: American Psychological Association.

Swan, L.A. 1976. "Black Families of Prisoners Research Report, 1973-1976." Nashville, Tenn.: Department of Sociology, Fisk University.

Sykes, G.M. 1958. *The Society of Captives*. Princeton: Princeton University Press.

Tapp, J.L., and Kohlberg, L. 1971. "Developing Senses of Law and Legal Justice." *Journal of Social Issues* 27(2):65-91.

Tapp, J.L., and Levine, F.J. 1970. "Persuasion to Virtue: A Preliminary Statement." *Law and Society Review* 4:565-582.

———. 1974. "Legal Socialization: Strategies for an Ethical Legality." *Stanford Law Review* 27:1-72.

Teeters, N.K. 1944. *World Penal Systems*. Philadelphia: Pennsylvania Prison Society.

———. 1946. *Penology from Panama to Cape Horn*. Philadelphia: University of Pennsylvania Press.

Torney, J.V. 1971. "Socialization of Attitudes toward the Legal System." *Journal of Social Issues* 27(2):137-154.

U.S. Department of Commerce, Bureau of the Census. 1973. *Persons in Institutions and Other Group Quarters*. Washington, D.C.: Department of Commerce.

U.S. Department of Justice, Federal Bureau of Investigation. 1979. *Crime in the United States, 1978*. Uniform Crime Reports. Washington, D.C.: Department of Justice.

Velimesis, M.L. 1969. "Criminal Justice for the Female Offender." *Journal of the American Association of University Women*.

Ward, D.A., and Kassebaum, G.C. 1965. *Women's Prison: Sex and Social Structure*. Chicago: Aldine Publishing.

Warren, M.Q. 1969. "The Case for Differential Treatment of Delinquents." *Annals of the American Academy of Political and Social Science*, vol. 381.

Yarrow, J. 1964. "Separation from Parents in Early Childhood." In M.L. Hoffman and L.N.W. Hoffman, eds. *Child Development Research*, vol. 1. New York: Russell Sage Foundation.

Zalba, S.R. 1964. *Women Prisoners and Their Families*. State of California Department of Social Welfare, Department of Corrections.

Zeitz, D. 1963. "Child Welfare Services in a Women's Correctional Institution." *Child Welfare* 42:185-190.

Zemans, E., and Cavan, R.S. 1958. "Marital Relationships of Prisoners." *Journal of Criminal Law, Criminology and Police Science* 49(1):50-57.

Zemans, E., and Cole, R.J. 1948. "Prison Babies." *The Mother*, no. 1, vol. 10.

Index

Index

About the Author

Ann M. Stanton is an associate professor of law at Arizona State University Law School. She has previously taught at the University of Santa Clara School of Law and the University of Minnesota and practiced law in California. She received the J.D. from Stanford Law School and the Ph.D. in psychology from Stanford University. Her research interests include family law and policy, juvenile law, and use of the social sciences in legislation and judicial decisions.